My Fun-Schooling Journal

Name:

Age:

Address:

Date:

Story Telling

Study 20
Fun and Interesting Topics

How to Earn Money

Nature Study

On-Line
Math
Tutorials

ART

Logic
GAMES

Library
Books

Life
Science

News
& World
Events

INSTRUCTIONS

Draw or list eight things that you want to learn about:

1.
2.
3.
4.
5.
6.
7.
8.

CHOOSE YOUR SCHOOL BOOKS

1. Go to the library, bookstore, a yard sale or your own book shelf.
2. Choose a big stack of interesting books about these topics and more. Choose books with photos and drawings.

Supplies Needed:

You will need pencils, colored pencils, a Bible, pens and markers.

Daily Plan: Use 4 to 10 pages each day.

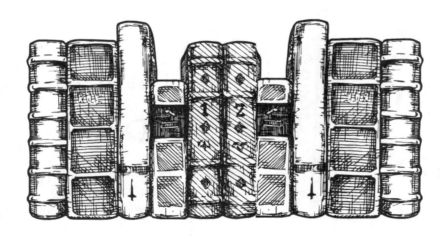

Library Books

1. Draw the cover of eight books that you will study this month.
2. Keep these books with this Journal.
3. You may use 4 to 10 pages each day in this journal.

What books are you reading today?

History Time

What is so important about today?

TODAY'S Date:_____

What was the most interesting or important thing that happened in the world on today's date in the past?

Instructions: If today is July 4th, you may write or draw about what happened on July 4, 1776. If today is September 11th, you may write about what happened on September 11, 2001.
(Need help: www.historynet.com/today-in-history)

Past Event:_____

_____

_____

_____

Color the continent where the event happened.

Yesterday's News

What was the most interesting or important thing that happened in the world yesterday?

HEADLINE:

_____

_____

WHO:_____

WHAT:_____

_____

WHEN:_____

WHERE:_____

WHY:_____

_____

_____

Draw It:

There are many ways to earn money.
Think about the job this person is doing.

Learning About Occupations

What is this person doing?

What skills are needed to do this job?

What would the world be like if no one did this job?

What kind of education does a person need to do this job?

On a scale of 1 to 10 would you like to have this job?

1 2 3 4 5 6 7 8 9 10

Meet the Classics - Copywork

Title:

Anne Of Green Gables

Author:

Lucy Maud Montgomery

Copy this paragraph onto the next page.

There are plenty of people in Avonlea and out of it, who can attend closely to their neighbor's business by dint of neglecting their own; but Mrs. Rachel Lynde was one of those capable creatures who can manage their own concerns and those of other folks into the bargain.

What's My Score?

Try to measure this Animal's abilities and characteristics. Circle a number for each ability. 10 means the animal is the best at a trait. 1 is the lowest score. For example, a cheetah would get 10 in running and a 1 in flying.

Swimming: 1 2 3 4 5 6 7 8 9 10
Jumping: 1 2 3 4 5 6 7 8 9 10
Running: 1 2 3 4 5 6 7 8 9 10
Hunting: 1 2 3 4 5 6 7 8 9 10
Hiding: 1 2 3 4 5 6 7 8 9 10
Climbing: 1 2 3 4 5 6 7 8 9 10
Flying: 1 2 3 4 5 6 7 8 9 10
Gliding: 1 2 3 4 5 6 7 8 9 10
Helping Humans: 1 2 3 4 5 6 7 8 9 10
Building: 1 2 3 4 5 6 7 8 9 10
Traveling: 1 2 3 4 5 6 7 8 9 10

What's My Score? _____

One word that best describes me:

_____

Thinking Time

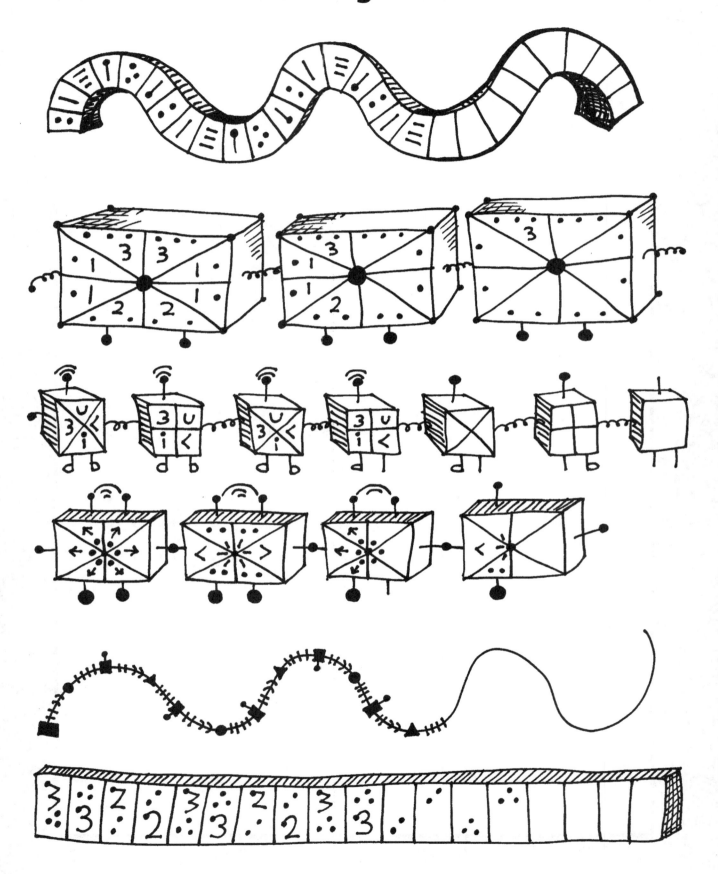

Nature Study

Go outside and make a realistic drawing of something you find in nature.

Story Time - What will happen next?
Draw the rest of the story.

Reading Time- Set a timer for 1 Hour

Read from four books in your stack.

Copy something from each book here.

Bible Time

Are you familiar with this story from the Bible?
Tell this story in your own words on the next page.

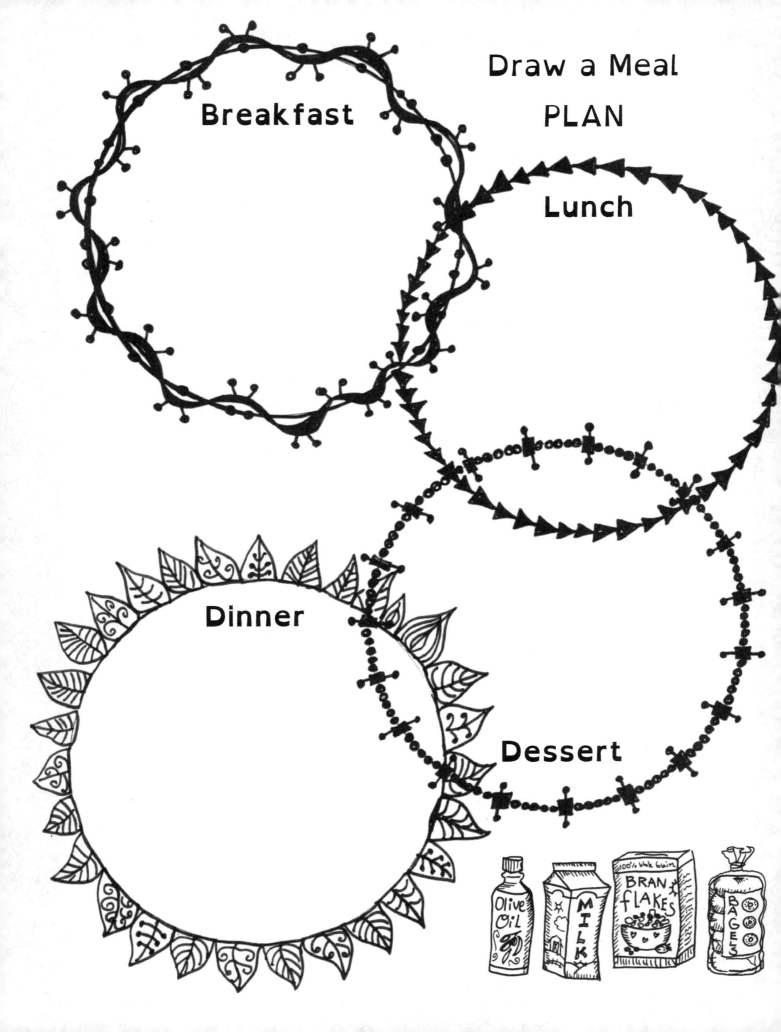

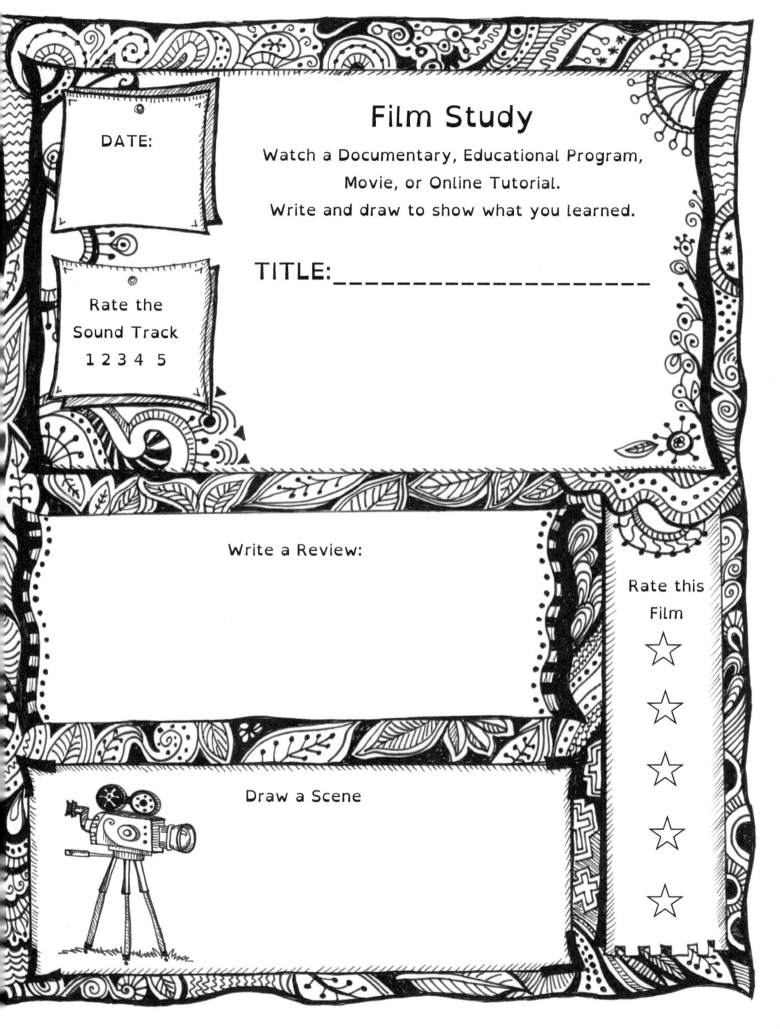

Draw the Missing Parts

Emotions & Moods

How are you feeling today?
Color the facial expressions to match today's moods.

List 3 things that might help you feel better.

1.
2.
3.

Drawing Time

Look through your library books
and find something to draw.

Spelling Time

Find 20 Words with **8** letters each.
Look in your books for words.
Write the words here:

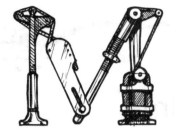

On-Line Math Time

Watch a Math Tutorial on-line
Use this paper to practice what you learn.
Try www.mathtrain.tv or www.khanacademy.org

Copywork

Find an interesting paragraph in one of your books and copy it. Be diligent to make your writing look exactly like it does in the book.

TITLE:_____

There are many ways to earn money.
Think about the job this person is doing.

I am a _____

Learning About Occupations

What is this person doing?

What skills are needed to do this job?

What would the world be like if no one did this job?

What kind of education does a person need to do this job?

On a scale of 1 to 10 would you like to have this job?

1 2 3 4 5 6 7 8 9 10

What books are you reading today?

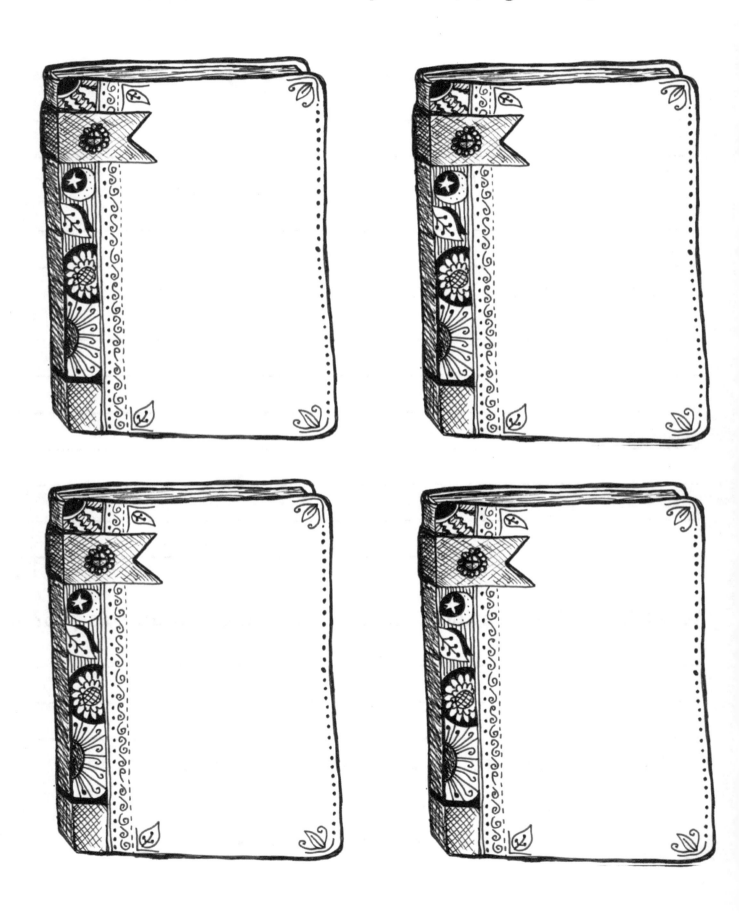

Thinking Time

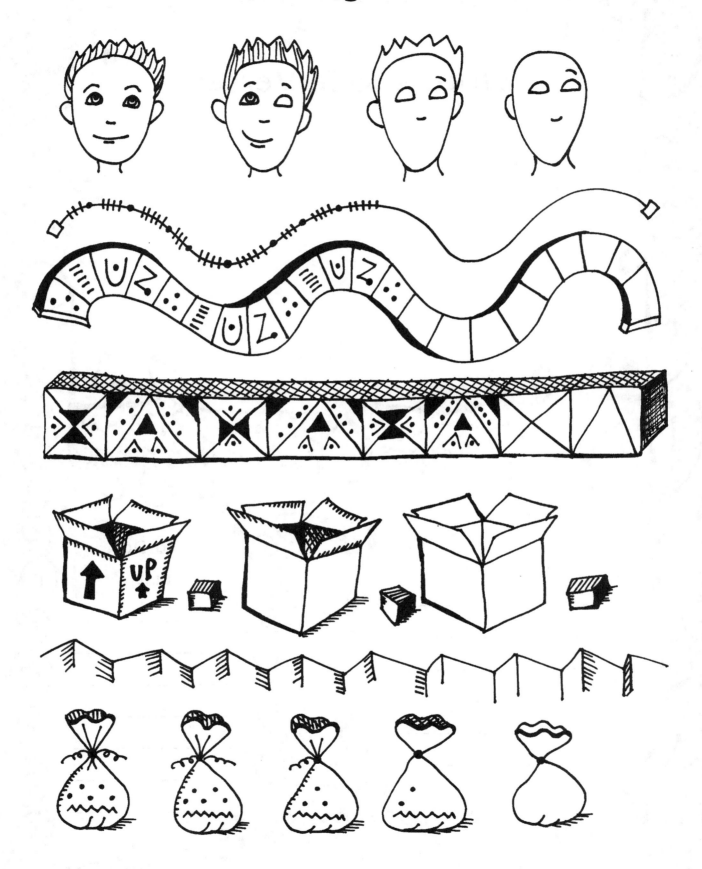

Nature Study

Go outside and make a realistic drawing of something you find in nature.

Story Time - What will happen next?
Draw the rest of the story.

Reading Time- Set a timer for 1 Hour

Read from four books in your stack.
Copy something from each book here.

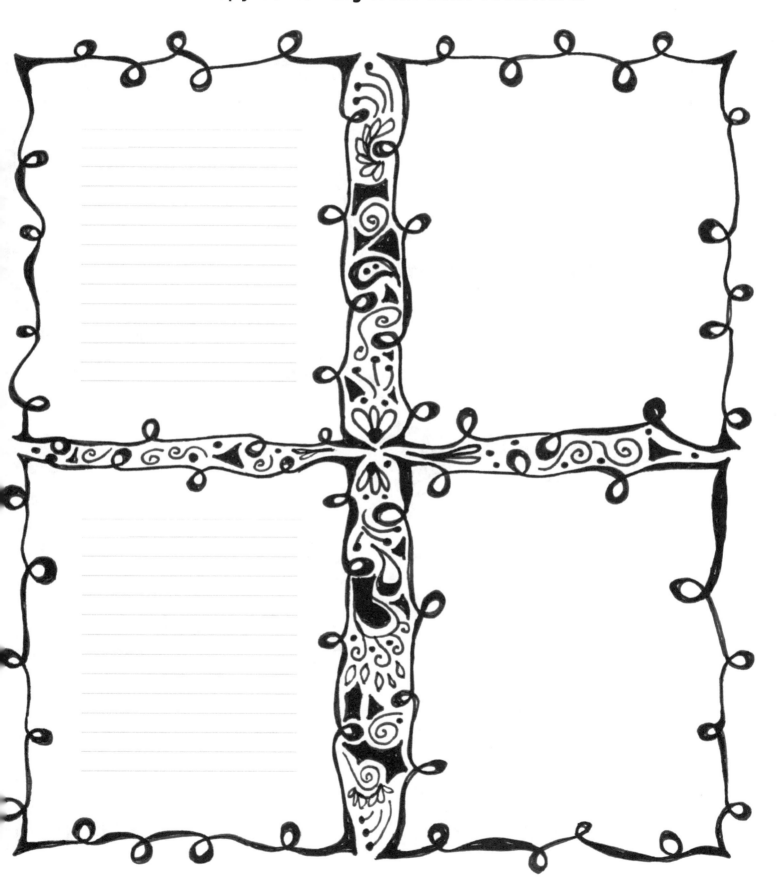

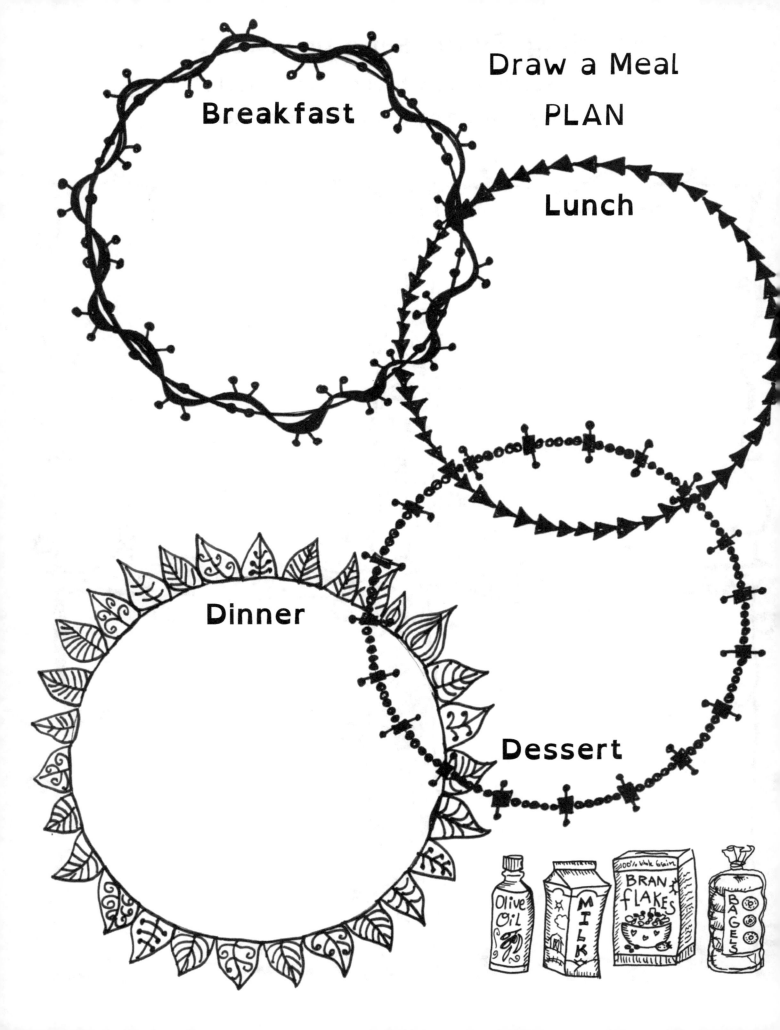

Film Study

DATE:

Rate the Sound Track
1 2 3 4 5

Watch a Documentary, Educational Program, Movie, or Online Tutorial.
Write and draw to show what you learned.

TITLE:_____

Write a Review:

Rate this Film
☆
☆
☆
☆
☆

Draw a Scene

History Time

What is so important about today?

TODAY'S Date:_____

What was the most interesting or important thing that happened in the world on today's date in the past?

Instructions: If today is July 4th, you may write or draw about what happened on July 4, 1776. If today is September 11th, you may write about what happened on September 11, 2001.
(Need help: www.historynet.com/today-in-history)

Past Event:_____
_____
_____
_____

Color the continent where the event happened.

Yesterday's News

What was the most interesting or important thing that happened in the world yesterday?

HEADLINE:

_____

_____

WHO: _____

WHAT: _____

WHEN: _____

WHERE: _____

WHY: _____

_____

_____

Draw It:

Spelling Time

Find 20 Words with 9 letters each.
Look in your books for words.
Write the words here:

Animal Quiz

How much do you know about this animal?

Can you draw the animal's habitat, food and enemies?

What's My Score?

Try to measure this Animal's abilities and characteristics. Circle a number for each ability. 10 means the animal is the best at a trait. 1 is the lowest score. For example, a cheetah would get 10 in running and a 1 in flying.

Swimming: 1 2 3 4 5 6 7 8 9 10
Jumping: 1 2 3 4 5 6 7 8 9 10
Running: 1 2 3 4 5 6 7 8 9 10
Hunting: 1 2 3 4 5 6 7 8 9 10
Hiding: 1 2 3 4 5 6 7 8 9 10
Climbing: 1 2 3 4 5 6 7 8 9 10
Flying: 1 2 3 4 5 6 7 8 9 10
Gliding: 1 2 3 4 5 6 7 8 9 10
Helping Humans: 1 2 3 4 5 6 7 8 9 10
Building: 1 2 3 4 5 6 7 8 9 10
Traveling: 1 2 3 4 5 6 7 8 9 10

What's My Score? _____

One word that best describes me:

_____

Emotions & Moods

How are you feeling today?
Color the facial expressions
to match today's moods.

List 3 things that might help you feel better.

1.
2.
3.

Drawing Time

Look through your library books
and find something to draw.

Bible Time

Are you familiar with this story from the Bible?
Tell this story in your own words on the next page.

Genesis 6

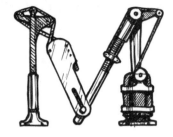

On-Line Math Time

Watch a Math Tutorial on-line

Use this paper to practice what you learn.

Try www.mathtrain.tv or www.khanacademy.org

Copywork

Find an interesting paragraph in one of your books and copy it. Be diligent to make your writing look exactly like it does in the book.

TITLE:_____

Listening Time

Listen to an audio book or classical music or ask someone to read a story to you while you color and draw on the next page.

What are you listening to?

_____

Meet the Classics - Copywork

Title:

Around the World in 80

Author:

Jules Verne

Copy this paragraph onto the next page.

Was Phileas Fogg rich? Undoubtedly. But those who knew him best could not imagine how he had made his fortune, and Mr. Fogg was the last person to whom to apply for the information. He was not lavish, nor, on the contrary, avaricious; for, whenever he knew that money was needed for a noble, useful, or benevolent purpose, he supplied it quietly and sometimes anonymously.

There are many ways to earn money.
Think about the job this person is doing.

I am a _____

Learning About Occupations

What is this person doing?

What skills are needed to do this job?

What would the world be like if no one did this job?

What kind of education does a person need to do this job?

On a scale of 1 to 10 would you like to have this job?

1 2 3 4 5 6 7 8 9 10

There are many ways to earn money.
Think about the job this person is doing.

I am a _____

Learning About Occupations

What is this person doing?

What skills are needed to do this job?

What would the world be like if no one did this job?

What kind of education does a person need to do this job?

On a scale of 1 to 10 would you like to have this job?

1 2 3 4 5 6 7 8 9 10

What books are you reading today?

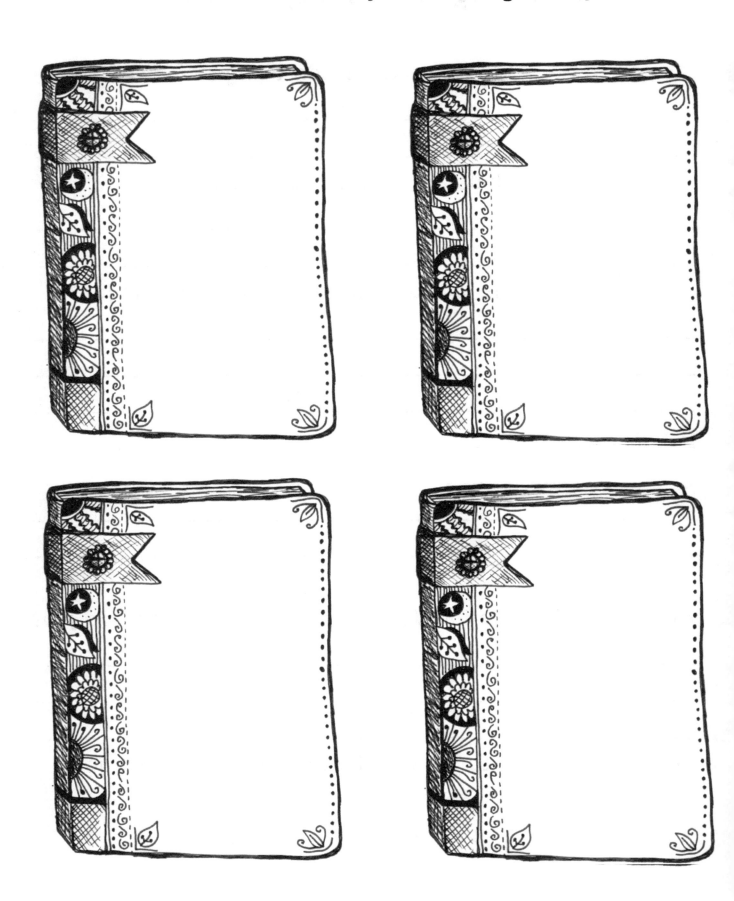

Thinking Time

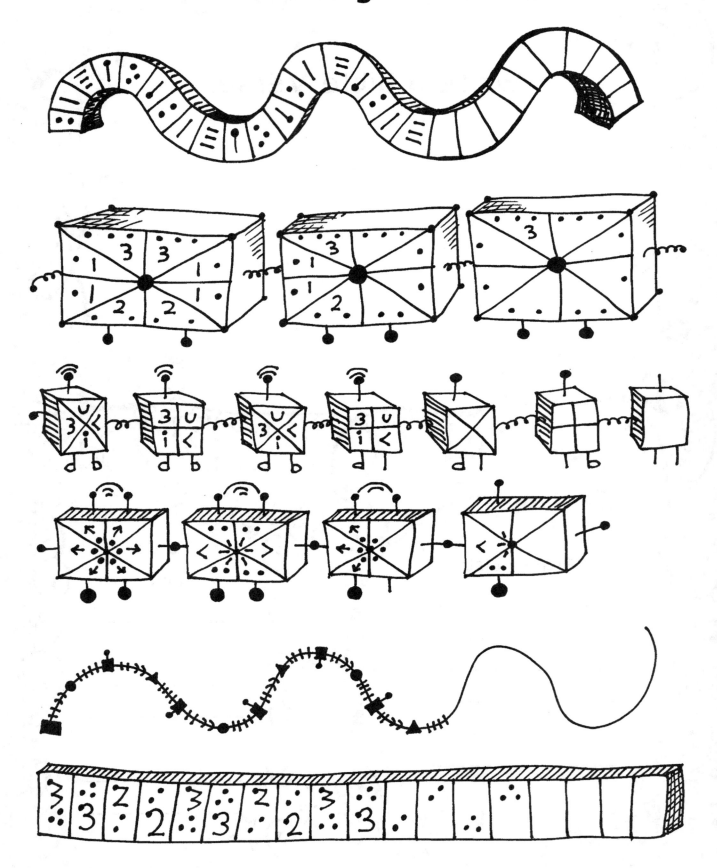

Nature Study

Go outside and make a realistic drawing of something you find in nature.

Story Time - What will happen next?
Draw the rest of the story.

Reading Time- Set a timer for 1 Hour
Read from four books in your stack.
Copy something from each book here.

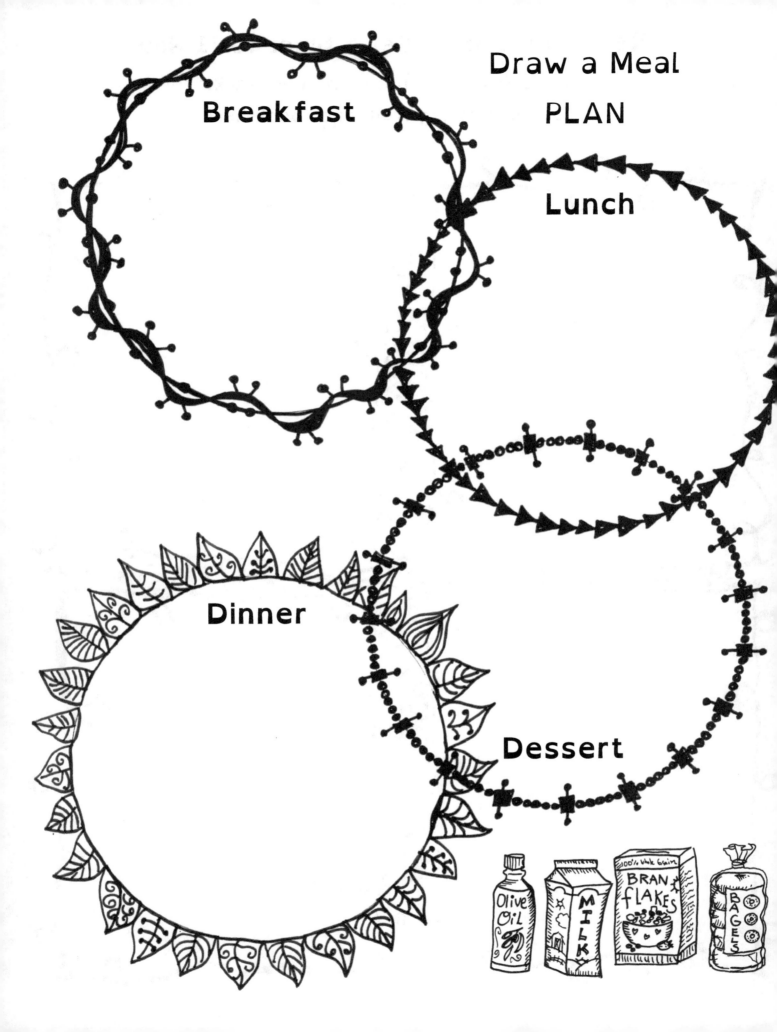

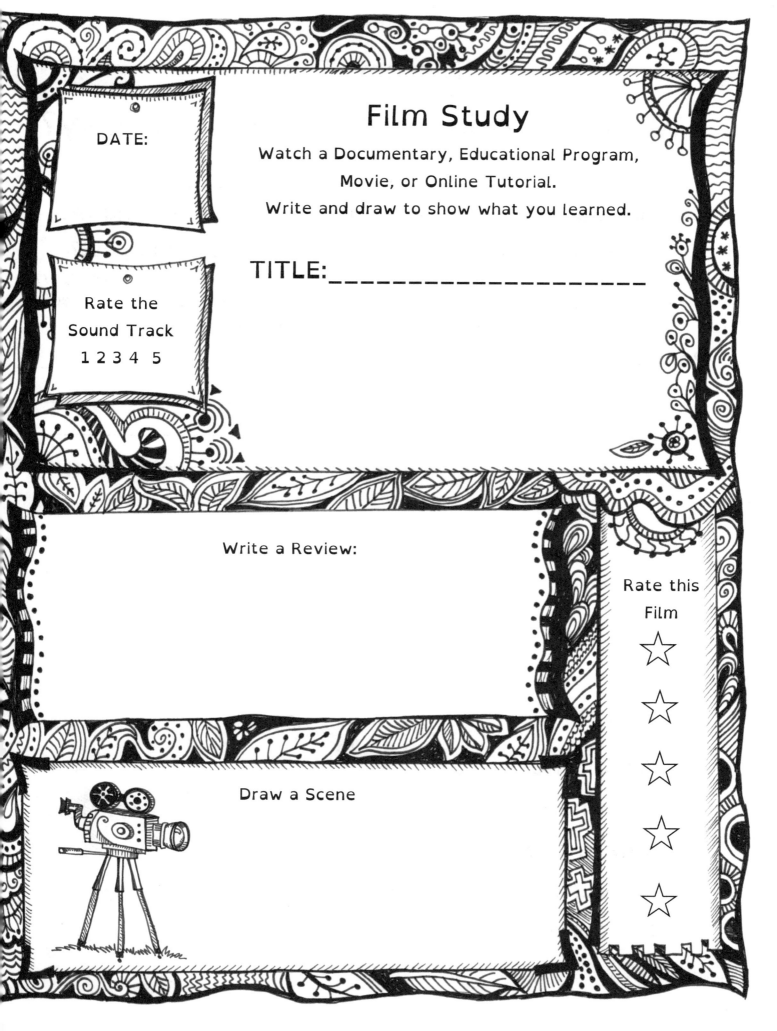

History Time

What is so important about today?

TODAY'S Date:_____

What was the most interesting or important thing that happened in the world on today's date in the past?

Instructions: If today is July 4th, you may write or draw about what happened on July 4, 1776. If today is September 11th, you may write about what happened on September 11, 2001.
(Need help: www.historynet.com/today-in-history)

Past Event:_____
_____
_____
_____

Color the continent where the event happened.

Yesterday's News

What was the most interesting or important thing that happened in the world yesterday?

HEADLINE:

_____

_____

WHO:_____

WHAT:_____

_____

WHEN:_____

WHERE:_____

WHY:_____

_____

_____

Draw It:

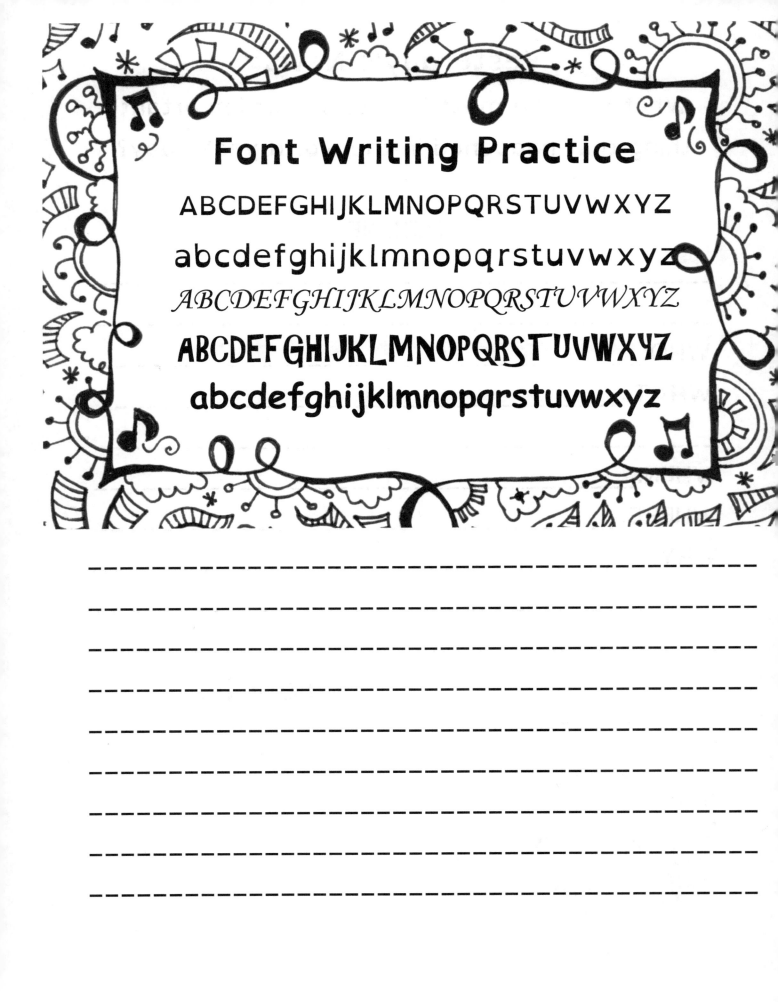

Spelling Time

Find 20 Words with ____ letters each.
Look in your books for words.
Write the words here:

_____   _____

_____   _____

_____   _____

_____   _____

_____   _____

_____   _____

_____   _____

_____   _____

_____   _____

_____   _____

There are many ways to earn money.
Think about the job this person is doing.

I am a _____

Learning About Occupations

What is this person doing?

What skills are needed to do this job?

What would the world be like if no one did this job?

What kind of education does a person need to do this job?

On a scale of 1 to 10 would you like to have this job?

1 2 3 4 5 6 7 8 9 10

What's My Score?

Try to measure this Animal's abilities and characteristics. Circle a number for each ability. 10 means the animal is the best at a trait. 1 is the lowest score. For example, a cheetah would get 10 in running and a 1 in flying.

Swimming: 1 2 3 4 5 6 7 8 9 10
Jumping: 1 2 3 4 5 6 7 8 9 10
Running: 1 2 3 4 5 6 7 8 9 10
Hunting: 1 2 3 4 5 6 7 8 9 10
Hiding: 1 2 3 4 5 6 7 8 9 10
Climbing: 1 2 3 4 5 6 7 8 9 10
Flying: 1 2 3 4 5 6 7 8 9 10
Gliding: 1 2 3 4 5 6 7 8 9 10
Helping Humans: 1 2 3 4 5 6 7 8 9 10
Building: 1 2 3 4 5 6 7 8 9 10
Traveling: 1 2 3 4 5 6 7 8 9 10

What's My Score? _____

One word that best describes me:

_____

Emotions & Moods

How are you feeling today?
Color the facial expressions
to match today's moods.

List 3 things that might help you feel better.

1.
2.
3.

Drawing Time

Look through your library books
and find something to draw.

Bible Time

Are you familiar with this story from the Bible?
Tell this story in your own words on the next page.

Luke 19

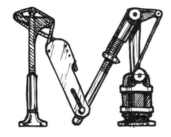

On-Line Math Time

Watch a Math Tutorial on-line
Use this paper to practice what you learn.
Try www.mathtrain.tv or www.khanacademy.org

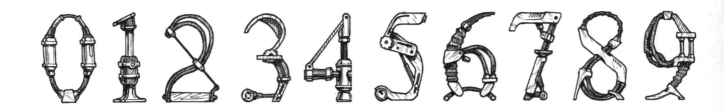

Copywork

Find an interesting paragraph in one of your books and copy it. Be diligent to make your writing look exactly like it does in the book.

TITLE:_____

Listening Time

Listen to an audio book or classical music or ask someone to read a story to you while you color and draw on the next page.

What are you listening to?

_____

Meet the Classics - Copywork

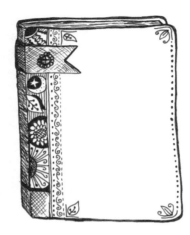

Title:

The Call of the Wild

Author:

Jack London

Copy this paragraph onto the next page.

Buck did not read the newspapers, or he would have known that trouble was brewing, not alone for himself, but for every tide-water dog, strong of muscle and with warm, long hair, from Puget Sound to San Diego.

There are many ways to earn money.
Think about the job this person is doing.

Railway employee

I am a _____

Learning About Occupations

What is this person doing?

What skills are needed to do this job?

What would the world be like if no one did this job?

What kind of education does a person need to do this job?

On a scale of 1 to 10 would you like to have this job?

1 2 3 4 5 6 7 8 9 10

There are many ways to earn money.
Think about the job this person is doing.

I am a _____

Learning About Occupations

What is this person doing?

What skills are needed to do this job?

What would the world be like if no one did this job?

What kind of education does a person need to do this job?

On a scale of 1 to 10 would you like to have this job?

1 2 3 4 5 6 7 8 9 10

What books are you reading today?

Thinking Time

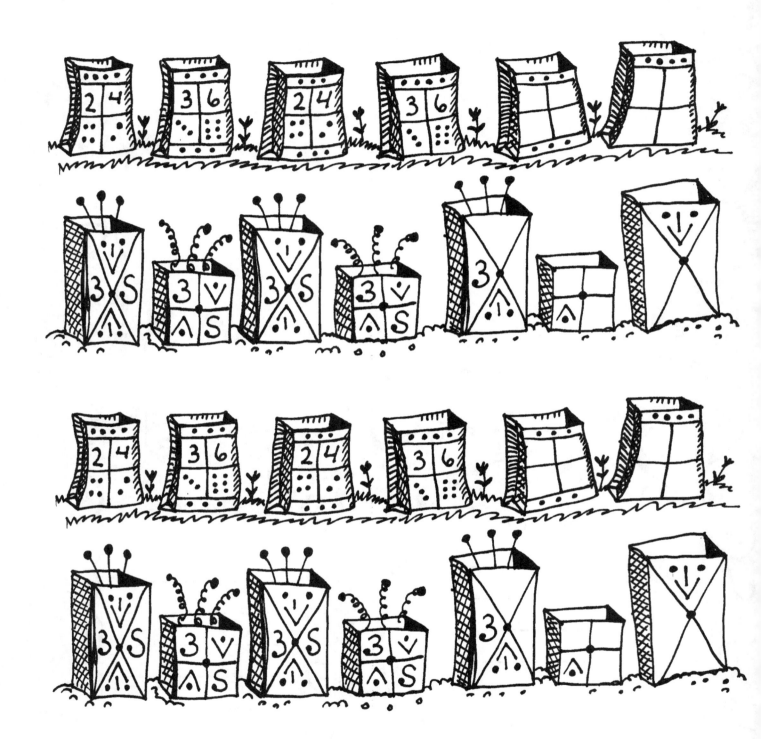

Nature Study
Go outside and make a realistic drawing of something you find in nature.

Story Time - What will happen next?
Draw the rest of the story.

Reading Time- Set a timer for 1 Hour

Read from four books in your stack.
Copy something from each book here.

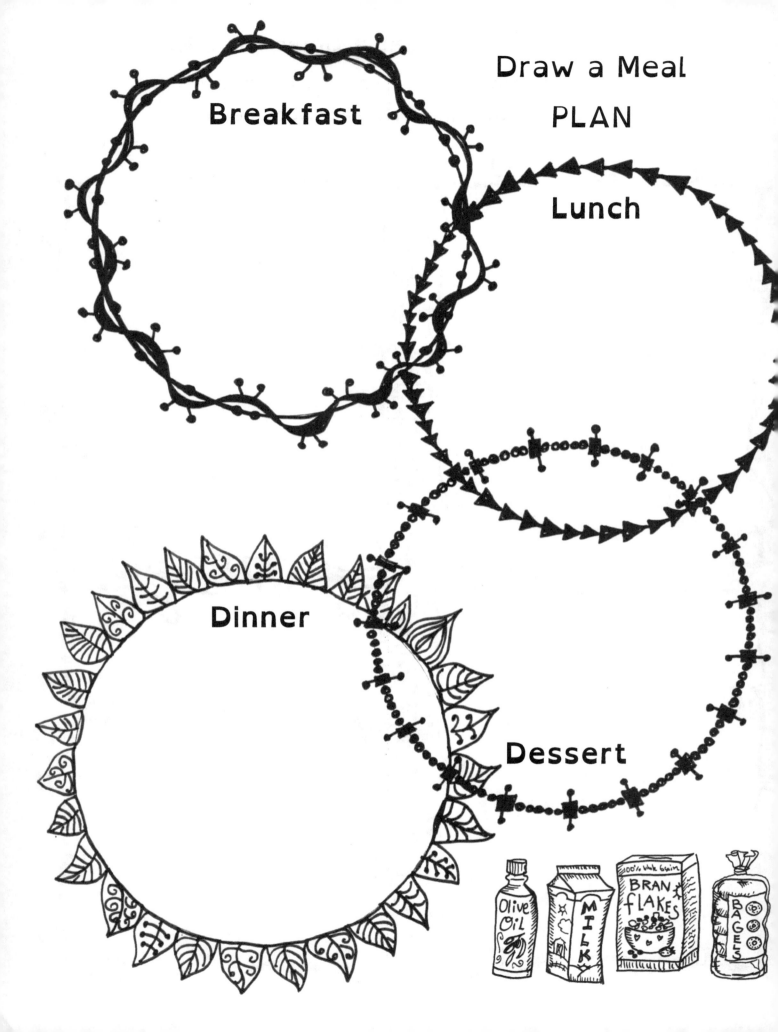

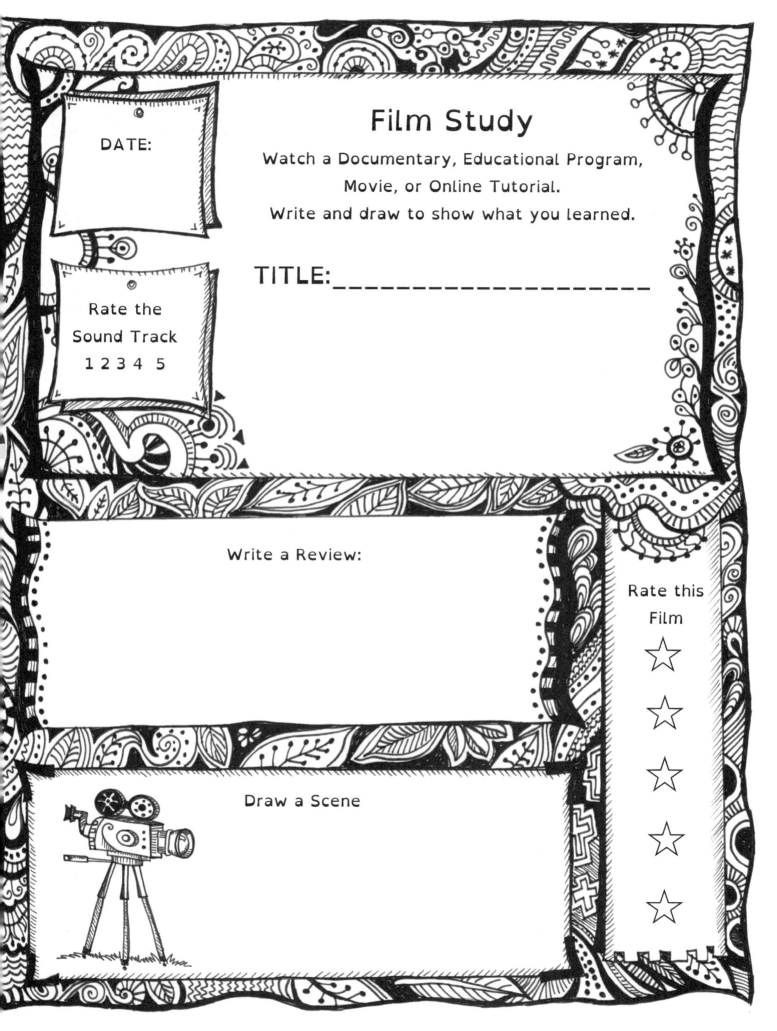

History Time

What is so important about today?

TODAY'S Date:_____

What was the most interesting or important thing that happened in the world on today's date in the past?

Instructions: If today is July 4th, you may write or draw about what happened on July 4, 1776. If today is September 11th, you may write about what happened on September 11, 2001.
(Need help: www.historynet.com/today-in-history)

Past Event:_____
_____
_____
_____

Color the continent where the event happened.

Yesterday's News

What was the most interesting or important thing that happened in the world yesterday?

HEADLINE:

_____

_____

WHO:_____

WHAT:_____

WHEN:_____

WHERE:_____

WHY:_____

_____

_____

Draw It:

Bible Time

Are you familiar with this story from the Bible?
Tell this story in your own words on the next page.

Luke 2

What's My Score?

Try to measure this Animal's abilities and characteristics. Circle a number for each ability. 10 means the animal is the best at a trait. 1 is the lowest score. For example, a cheetah would get 10 in running and a 1 in flying.

Swimming: 1 2 3 4 5 6 7 8 9 10
Jumping: 1 2 3 4 5 6 7 8 9 10
Running: 1 2 3 4 5 6 7 8 9 10
Hunting: 1 2 3 4 5 6 7 8 9 10
Hiding: 1 2 3 4 5 6 7 8 9 10
Climbing: 1 2 3 4 5 6 7 8 9 10
Flying: 1 2 3 4 5 6 7 8 9 10
Gliding: 1 2 3 4 5 6 7 8 9 10
Helping Humans: 1 2 3 4 5 6 7 8 9 10
Building: 1 2 3 4 5 6 7 8 9 10
Traveling: 1 2 3 4 5 6 7 8 9 10

What's My Score? _____

One word that best describes me:

_____

Emotions & Moods

How are you feeling today?
Color the facial expressions
to match today's moods.

List 3 things that might help you feel better.

1.
2.
3.

Drawing Time

Look through your library books
and find something to draw.

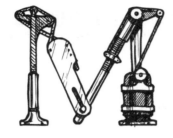

On-Line Math Time

Watch a Math Tutorial on-line
Use this paper to practice what you learn.
Try www.mathtrain.tv or www.khanacademy.org

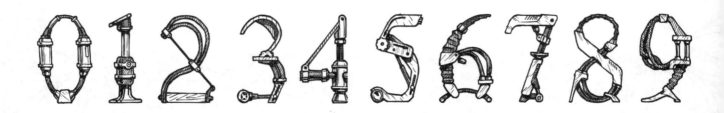

Copywork

Find an interesting paragraph in one of your books and copy it. Be diligent to make your writing look exactly like it does in the book.

TITLE:_____

Listening Time

Listen to an audio book or classical music or ask someone to read a story to you while you color and draw on the next page.

What are you listening to?

_____

Meet the Classics - Copywork

Title:

Common Sense

Author:

Thomas Paine

Copy this paragraph onto the next page.

In order to gain a clear and just idea of the design and end of government, let us suppose a small number of persons settled in some sequestered part of the earth, unconnected with the rest, they will then represent the first peopling of any country, or of the world. In this state of natural liberty, society will be their first thought.

There are many ways to earn money.
Think about the job this person is doing.

I am a _____

Learning About Occupations

What is this person doing?

What skills are needed to do this job?

What would the world be like if no one did this job?

What kind of education does a person need to do this job?

On a scale of 1 to 10 would you like to have this job?

1 2 3 4 5 6 7 8 9 10

There are many ways to earn money.
Think about the job this person is doing.

I am a _____

Learning About Occupations

What is this person doing?

What skills are needed to do this job?

What would the world be like if no one did this job?

What kind of education does a person need to do this job?

On a scale of 1 to 10 would you like to have this job?

1 2 3 4 5 6 7 8 9 10

What books are you reading today?

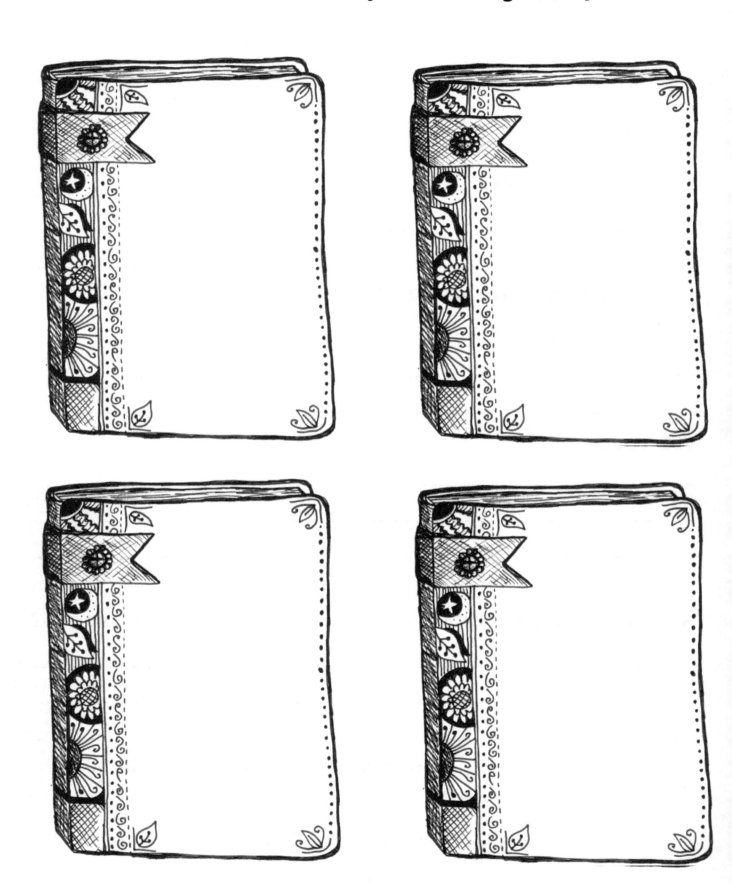

Thinking Time

Nature Study

Go outside and make a realistic drawing of something you find in nature.

Story Time - What will happen next?
Draw the rest of the story.

Reading Time- Set a timer for 1 Hour

Read from four books in your stack.
Copy something from each book here.

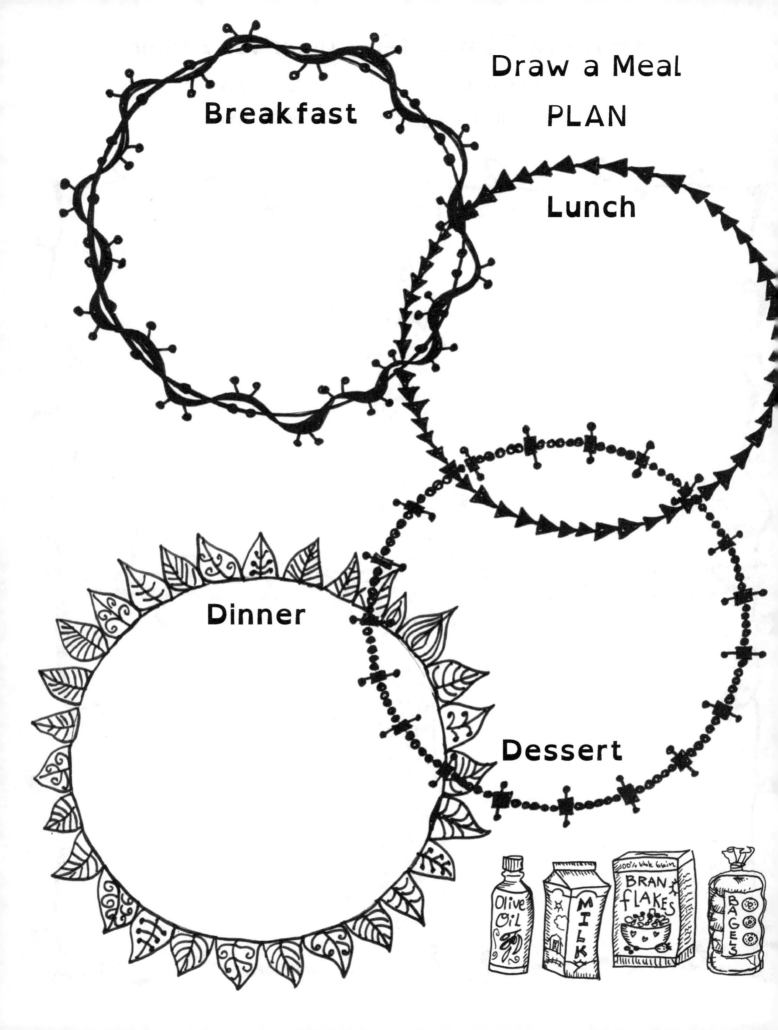

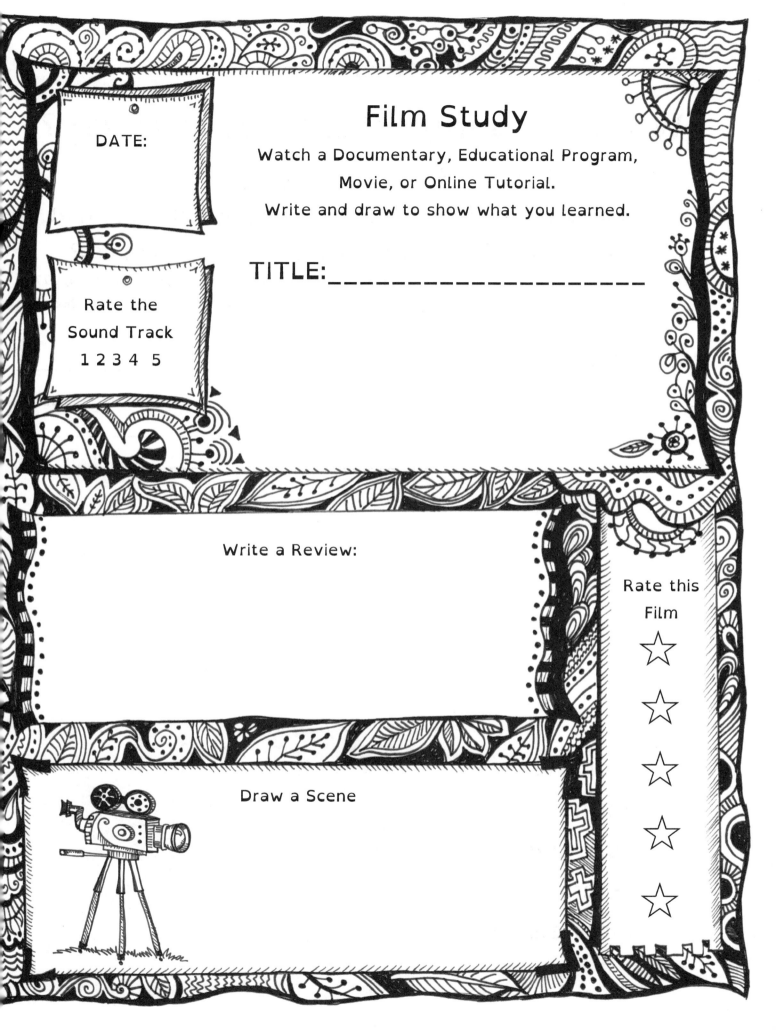

History Time

What is so important about today?

TODAY'S Date:_____

What was the most interesting or important thing that happened in the world on today's date in the past?

Instructions: If today is July 4th, you may write or draw about what happened on July 4, 1776. If today is September 11th, you may write about what happened on September 11, 2001.
(Need help: www.historynet.com/today-in-history)

Past Event:_____
_____
_____
_____

Color the continent where the event happened.

Yesterday's News

What was the most interesting or important thing that happened in the world yesterday?

HEADLINE:

_____

_____

WHO:_____

WHAT:_____

_____

WHEN:_____

WHERE:_____

WHY:_____

_____

_____

Draw It:

Spelling Time

Find 20 Words with ____ letters each.
Look in your books for words.
Write the words here:

What's My Score?

Try to measure this Animal's abilities and characteristics. Circle a number for each ability. 10 means the animal is the best at a trait. 1 is the lowest score. For example, a cheetah would get 10 in running and a 1 in flying.

Swimming: 1 2 3 4 5 6 7 8 9 10
Jumping: 1 2 3 4 5 6 7 8 9 10
Running: 1 2 3 4 5 6 7 8 9 10
Hunting: 1 2 3 4 5 6 7 8 9 10
Hiding: 1 2 3 4 5 6 7 8 9 10
Climbing: 1 2 3 4 5 6 7 8 9 10
Flying: 1 2 3 4 5 6 7 8 9 10
Gliding: 1 2 3 4 5 6 7 8 9 10
Helping Humans: 1 2 3 4 5 6 7 8 9 10
Building: 1 2 3 4 5 6 7 8 9 10
Traveling: 1 2 3 4 5 6 7 8 9 10

What's My Score? _____

One word that best describes me:

_____

Bible Time

Are you familiar with this story from the Bible?
Tell this story in your own words on the next page.

Ruth 1 – 4

Emotions & Moods

How are you feeling today? Color the facial expressions to match today's moods.

List 3 things that might help you feel better.

1.
2.
3.

Drawing Time

Look through your library books
and find something to draw.

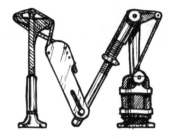

On-Line Math Time

Watch a Math Tutorial on-line
Use this paper to practice what you learn.
Try www.mathtrain.tv or www.khanacademy.org

Copywork

Find an interesting paragraph in one of your books and copy it. Be diligent to make your writing look exactly like it does in the book.

TITLE:_____

Listening Time

Listen to an audio book or classical music or ask someone to read a story to you while you color and draw on the next page.

What are you listening to?

_____

Meet the Classics - Copywork

Title:

Hard Times

Author:

Charles Dickens

Copy this paragraph onto the next page.

'NOW, what I want is, Facts. Teach these boys and girls nothing but Facts. Facts alone are wanted in life. Plant nothing else, and root out everything else. You can only form the minds of reasoning animals upon Facts: nothing else will ever be of any service to them. This is the principle on which I bring up my own children, and this is the principle on which I bring up these children. Stick to Facts, sir!'

There are many ways to earn money.
Think about the job this person is doing.

I am a _____

Learning About Occupations

What is this person doing?

What skills are needed to do this job?

What would the world be like if no one did this job?

What kind of education does a person need to do this job?

On a scale of 1 to 10 would you like to have this job?

1 2 3 4 5 6 7 8 9 10

There are many ways to earn money.
Think about the job this person is doing.

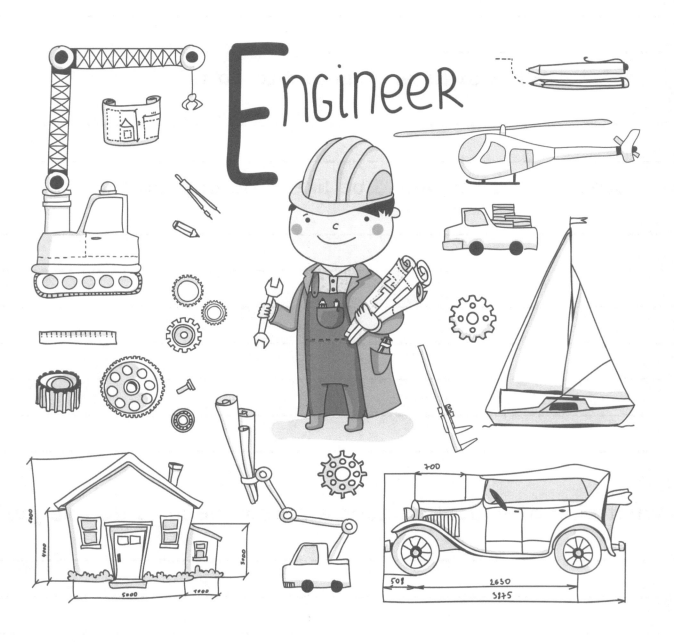

I am a _____

Learning About Occupations

What is this person doing?

What skills are needed to do this job?

What would the world be like if no one did this job?

What kind of education does a person need to do this job?

On a scale of 1 to 10 would you like to have this job?

1 2 3 4 5 6 7 8 9 10

What books are you reading today?

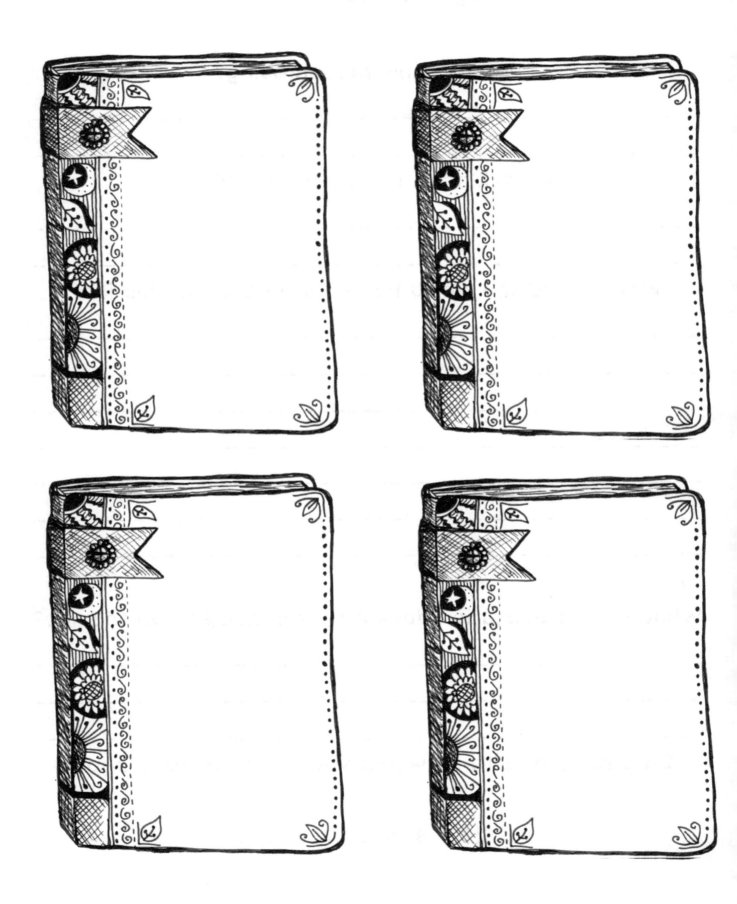

Thinking Time

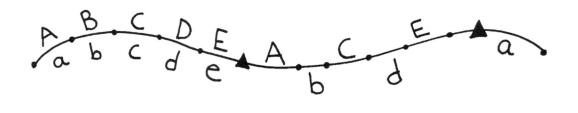

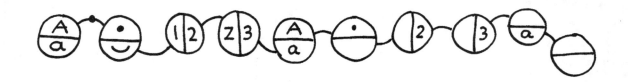
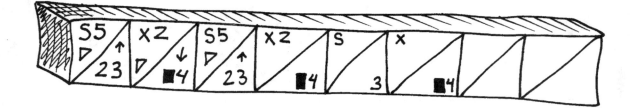
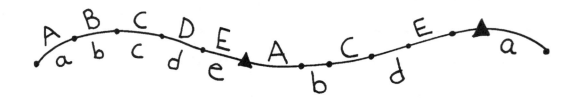

Nature Study

Go outside and make a realistic drawing of something you find in nature.

Story Time - What will happen next?
Draw the rest of the story.

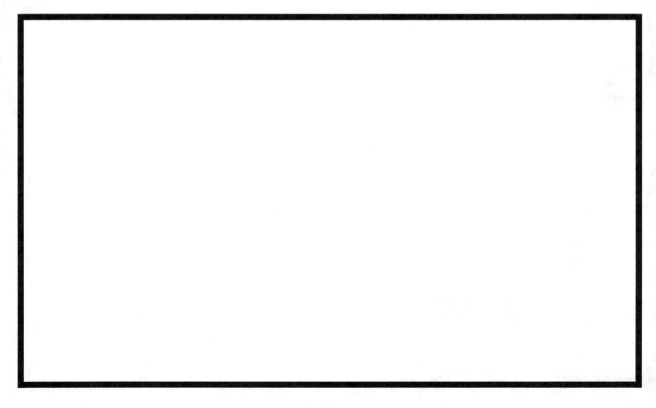

Reading Time- Set a timer for 1 Hour
Read from four books in your stack.
Copy something from each book here.

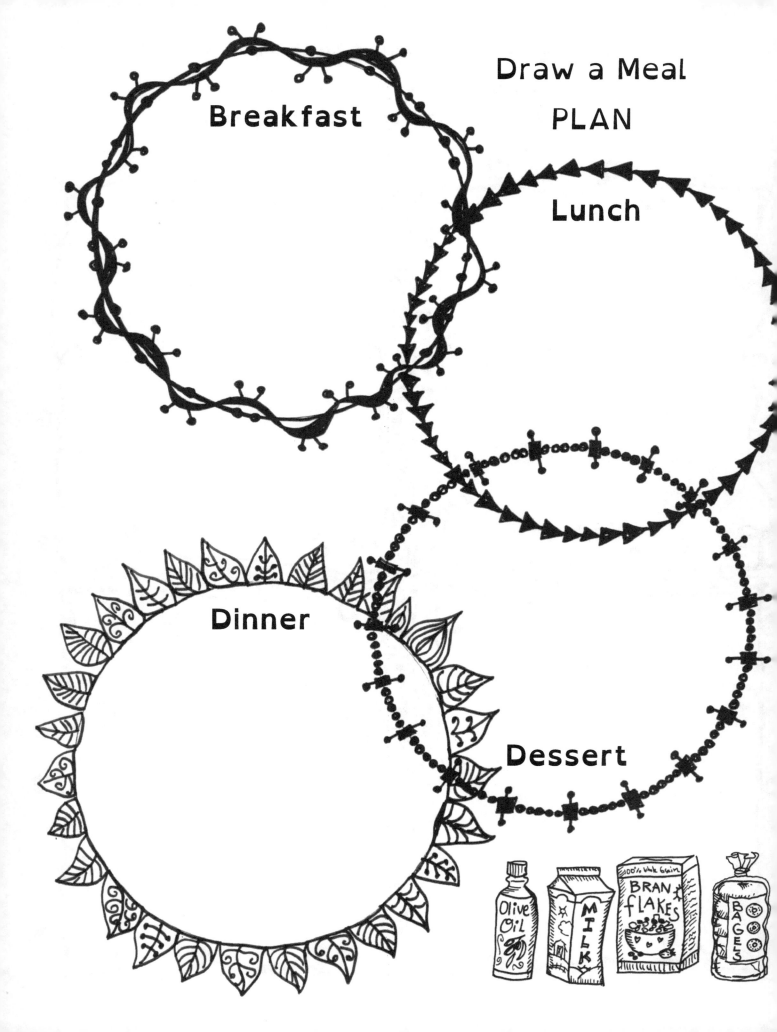

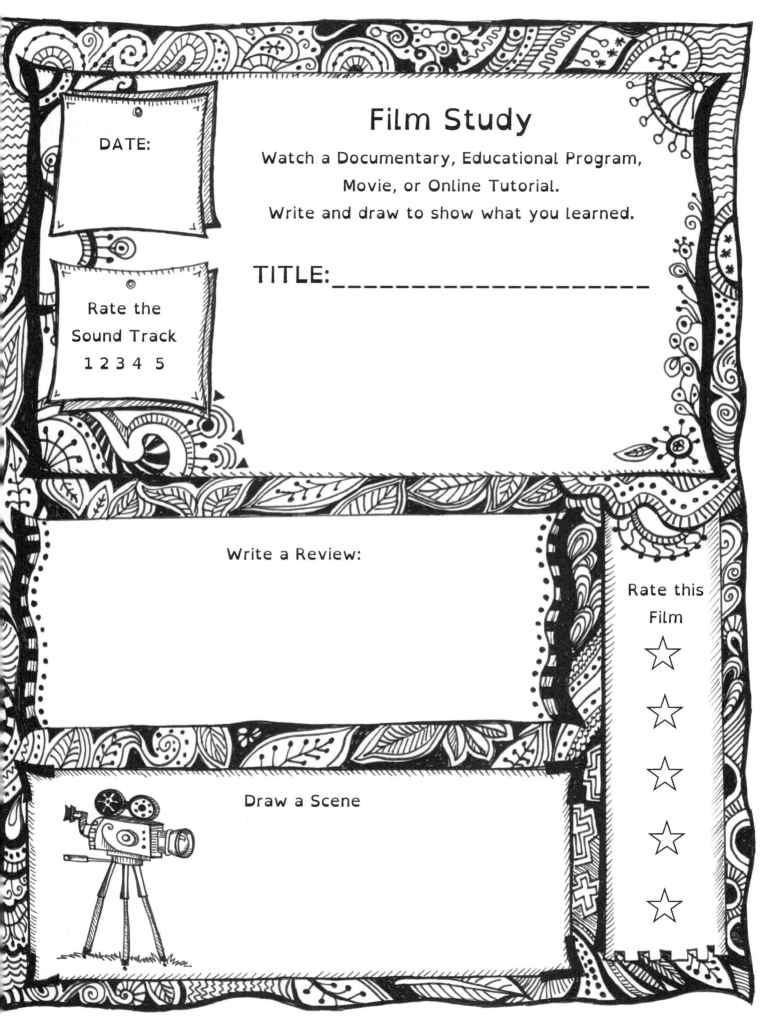

History Time

What is so important about today?

TODAY'S Date:_____

What was the most interesting or important thing that happened in the world on today's date in the past?

Instructions: If today is July 4th, you may write or draw about what happened on July 4, 1776. If today is September 11th, you may write about what happened on September 11, 2001.
(Need help: www.historynet.com/today-in-history)

Past Event:_____
_____
_____
_____

Color the continent where the event happened.

Yesterday's News

What was the most interesting or important thing that happened in the world yesterday?

HEADLINE:

_____

_____

WHO:_____

WHAT:_____

_____

WHEN:_____

WHERE:_____

WHY:_____

_____

_____

Draw It:

Spelling Time

Find 20 Words with 7 letters each.
Look in your books for words.
Write the words here:

Animal Quiz

How much do you know about this animal?

Can you draw the animal's habitat, food and enemies?

What's My Score?

Try to measure this Animal's abilities and characteristics. Circle a number for each ability. 10 means the animal is the best at a trait. 1 is the lowest score. For example, a cheetah would get 10 in running and a 1 in flying.

Swimming: 1 2 3 4 5 6 7 8 9 10
Jumping: 1 2 3 4 5 6 7 8 9 10
Running: 1 2 3 4 5 6 7 8 9 10
Hunting: 1 2 3 4 5 6 7 8 9 10
Hiding: 1 2 3 4 5 6 7 8 9 10
Climbing: 1 2 3 4 5 6 7 8 9 10
Flying: 1 2 3 4 5 6 7 8 9 10
Gliding: 1 2 3 4 5 6 7 8 9 10
Helping Humans: 1 2 3 4 5 6 7 8 9 10
Building: 1 2 3 4 5 6 7 8 9 10
Traveling: 1 2 3 4 5 6 7 8 9 10

What's My Score? _____

One word that best describes me:

_____

Emotions & Moods

How are you feeling today?
Color the facial expressions
to match today's moods.

List 3 things that might help you feel better.

1.
2.
3.

Drawing Time

Look through your library books
and find something to draw.

Bible Time

Are you familiar with this story from the Bible?
Tell this story in your own words on the next page.

Genesis 1 and 2

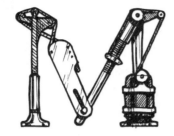

On-Line Math Time

Watch a Math Tutorial on-line
Use this paper to practice what you learn.
Try www.mathtrain.tv or www.khanacademy.org

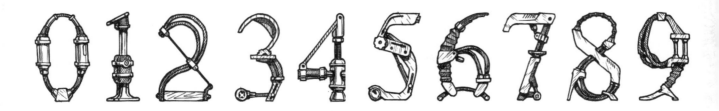

Copywork

Find an interesting paragraph in one of your books and copy it. Be diligent to make your writing look exactly like it does in the book.

TITLE:_____

Meet the Classics - Copywork

Title:

Little Lord Fauntleroy

Author:

Frances Hodgson Burnett

Copy this paragraph onto the next page.

Cedric himself knew nothing whatever about it. It had never been even mentioned to him. He knew that his papa had been an Englishman, because his mamma had told him so; but then his papa had died when he was so little a boy that he could not remember very much about him, except that he was big, and had blue eyes and a long mustache, and that it was a splendid thing to be carried around the room on his shoulder

There are many ways to earn money.
Think about the job this person is doing.

I am a _____

Learning About Occupations

What is this person doing?

What skills are needed to do this job?

What would the world be like if no one did this job?

What kind of education does a person need to do this job?

On a scale of 1 to 10 would you like to have this job?

1 2 3 4 5 6 7 8 9 10

There are many ways to earn money.
Think about the job this person is doing.

I am a _____

Learning About Occupations

What is this person doing?

What skills are needed to do this job?

What would the world be like if no one did this job?

What kind of education does a person need to do this job?

On a scale of 1 to 10 would you like to have this job?

1 2 3 4 5 6 7 8 9 10

What books are you reading today?

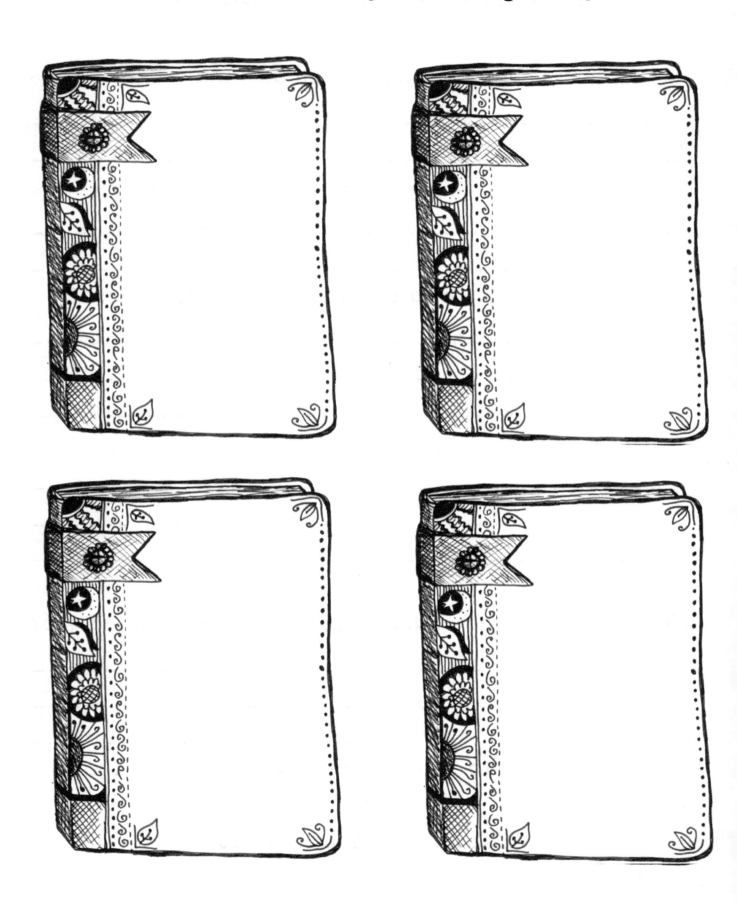

Thinking Time

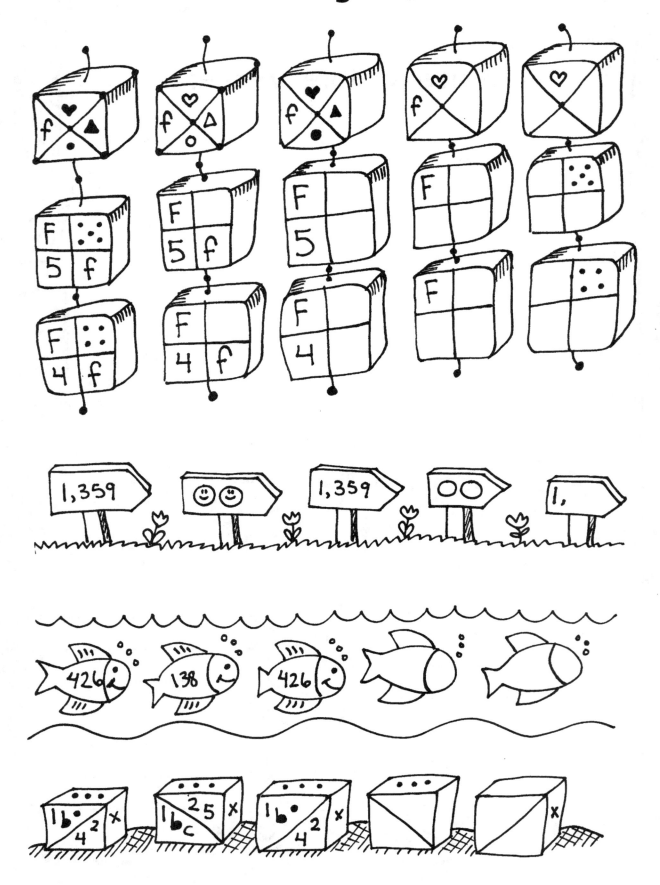

Nature Study

Go outside and make a realistic drawing of something you find in nature.

Story Time - What will happen next?
Draw the rest of the story.

Reading Time- Set a timer for 1 Hour

Read from four books in your stack.
Copy something from each book here.

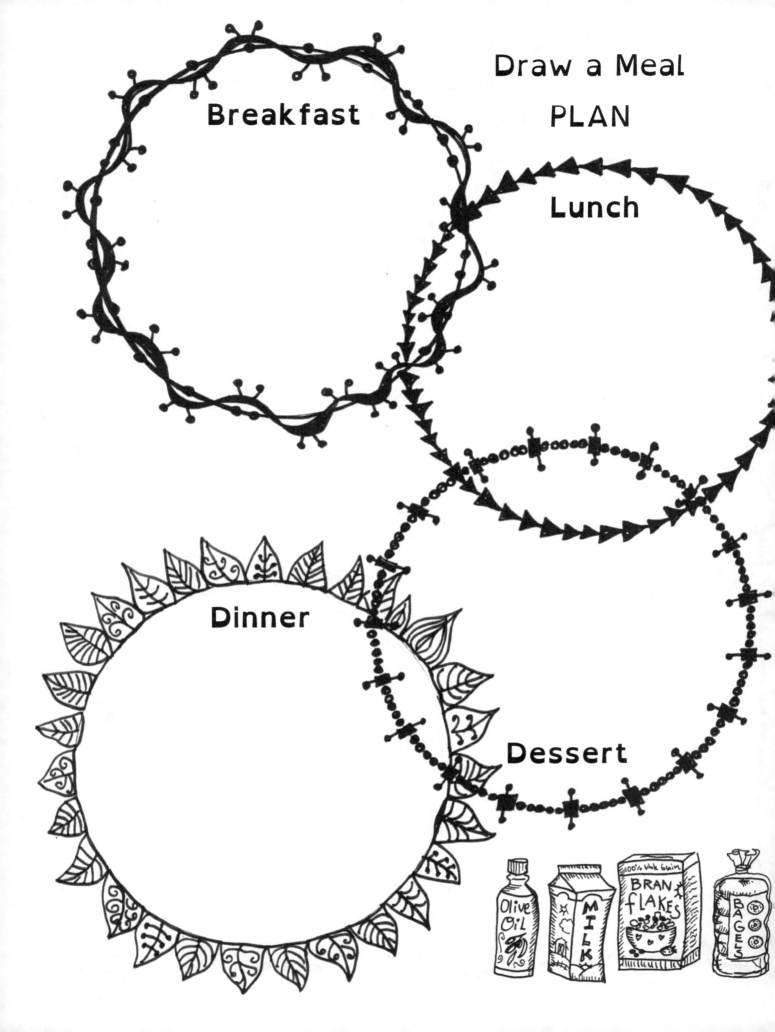

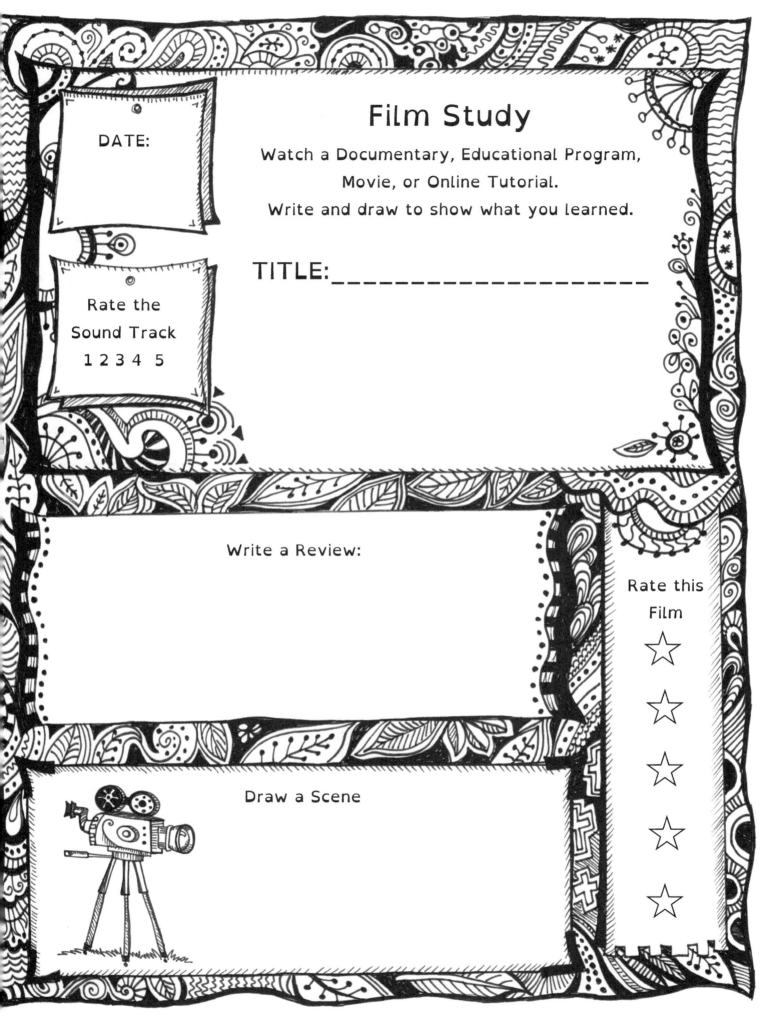

History Time

What is so important about today?

TODAY'S Date:_____

What was the most interesting or important thing that happened in the world on today's date in the past?

Instructions: If today is July 4th, you may write or draw about what happened on July 4, 1776. If today is September 11th, you may write about what happened on September 11, 2001.
(Need help: www.historynet.com/today-in-history)

Past Event:_____
_____
_____
_____

Color the continent where the event happened.

Yesterday's News

What was the most interesting or important thing that happened in the world yesterday?

HEADLINE:

_____

_____

WHO: _____

WHAT: _____

_____

WHEN: _____

WHERE: _____

WHY: _____

_____

_____

Draw It:

Font Writing Practice

ABCDEFGHIJKLMNOPQRSTUVWXYZ

abcdefghijklmnopqrstuvwxyz

ABCDEFGHIJKLMNOPQRSTUVWXYZ

ABCDEFGHIJKLMNOPQRSTUVWXYZ

abcdefghijklmnopqrstuvwxyz

Spelling Time

Find 20 Words with 8 letters each.
Look in your books for words.
Write the words here:

Animal Quiz

How much do you know about this animal?

Can you draw the animal's habitat, food and enemies?

What's My Score?

Try to measure this Animal's abilities and characteristics. Circle a number for each ability. 10 means the animal is the best at a trait. 1 is the lowest score. For example, a cheetah would get 10 in running and a 1 in flying.

Swimming: 1 2 3 4 5 6 7 8 9 10
Jumping: 1 2 3 4 5 6 7 8 9 10
Running: 1 2 3 4 5 6 7 8 9 10
Hunting: 1 2 3 4 5 6 7 8 9 10
Hiding: 1 2 3 4 5 6 7 8 9 10
Climbing: 1 2 3 4 5 6 7 8 9 10
Flying: 1 2 3 4 5 6 7 8 9 10
Gliding: 1 2 3 4 5 6 7 8 9 10
Helping Humans: 1 2 3 4 5 6 7 8 9 10
Building: 1 2 3 4 5 6 7 8 9 10
Traveling: 1 2 3 4 5 6 7 8 9 10

What's My Score? _____

One word that best describes me:

_____

Bible Time

Are you familiar with this story from the Bible?
Tell this story in your own words on the next page.

Emotions & Moods

How are you feeling today?
Color the facial expressions
to match today's moods.

List 3 things that might help you feel better.

1.
2.
3.

Drawing Time

Look through your library books
and find something to draw.

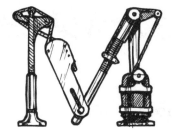

On-Line Math Time

Watch a Math Tutorial on-line
Use this paper to practice what you learn.
Try www.mathtrain.tv or www.khanacademy.org

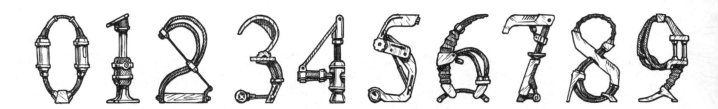

Copywork

Find an interesting paragraph in one of your books and copy it. Be diligent to make your writing look exactly like it does in the book.

TITLE:_____

Listening Time

Listen to an audio book or classical music or ask someone to read a story to you while you color and draw on the next page.

What are you listening to?

_____

Meet the Classics - Copywork

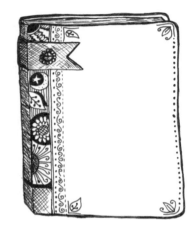

Title:
The Secret Garden

Author:
Frances Hodgson Burnett

Copy this paragraph onto the next page.

There was something mysterious in the air that morning. Nothing was done in its regular order and several of the native servants seemed missing, while those whom Mary saw slunk or hurried about with ashy and scared faces. But no one would tell her anything and her Ayah did not come.

There are many ways to earn money.
Think about the job this person is doing.

I am a _____

Learning About Occupations

What is this person doing?

What skills are needed to do this job?

What would the world be like if no one did this job?

What kind of education does a person need to do this job?

On a scale of 1 to 10 would you like to have this job?

1 2 3 4 5 6 7 8 9 10

There are many ways to earn money.
Think about the job this person is doing.

Chemist

I am a _____

Learning About Occupations

What is this person doing?

What skills are needed to do this job?

What would the world be like if no one did this job?

What kind of education does a person need to do this job?

On a scale of 1 to 10 would you like to have this job?

1 2 3 4 5 6 7 8 9 10

What books are you reading today?

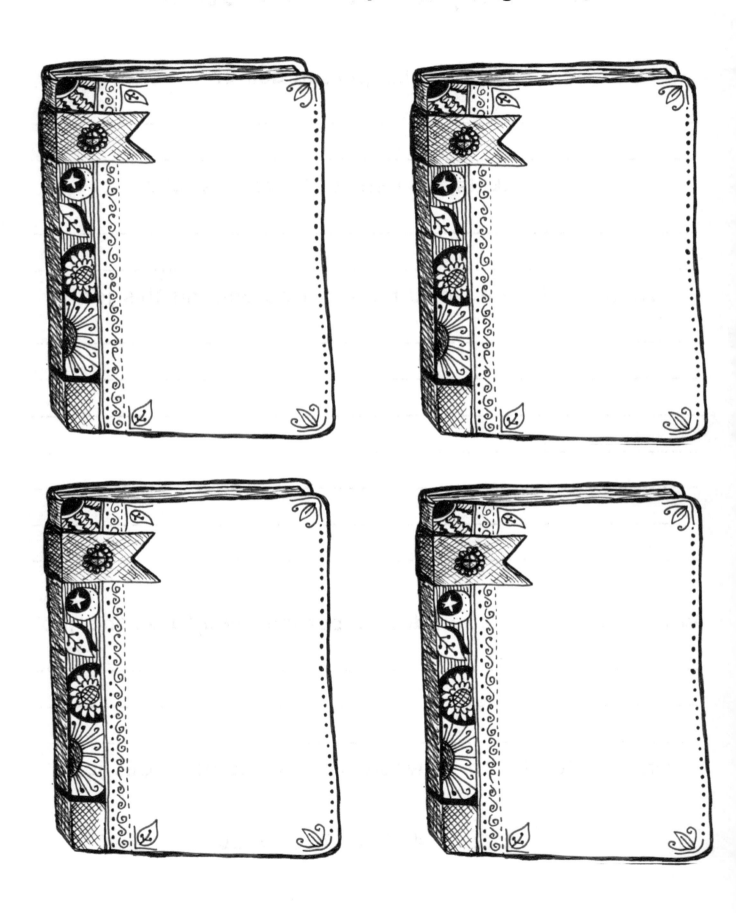

Thinking Time

Nature Study

Go outside and make a realistic drawing of something you find in nature.

Story Time - What will happen next?
Draw the rest of the story.

Reading Time- Set a timer for 1 Hour
Read from four books in your stack.
Copy something from each book here.

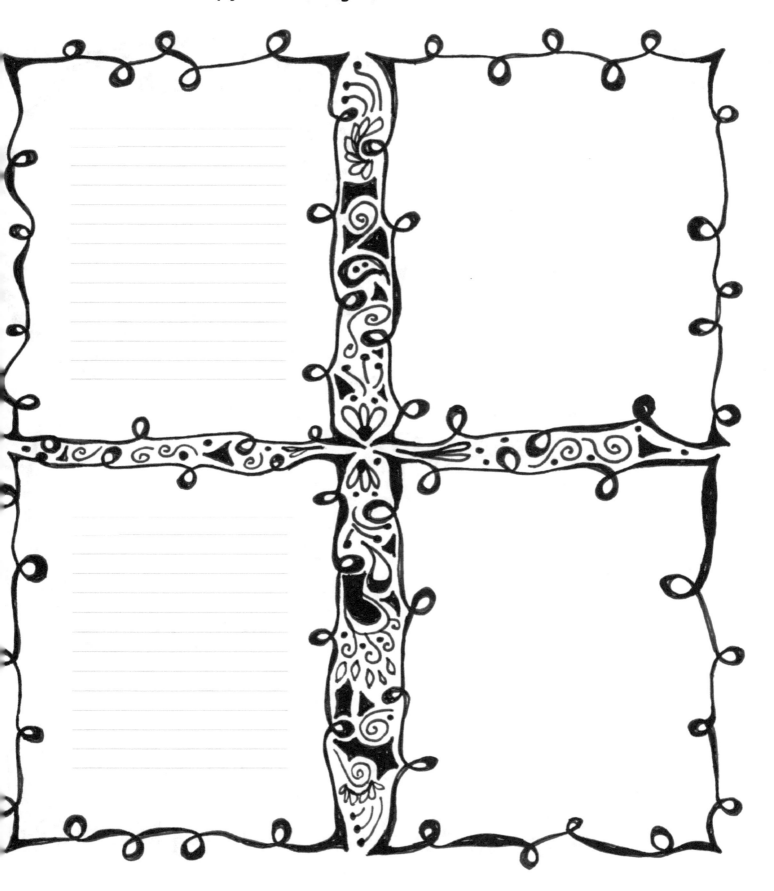

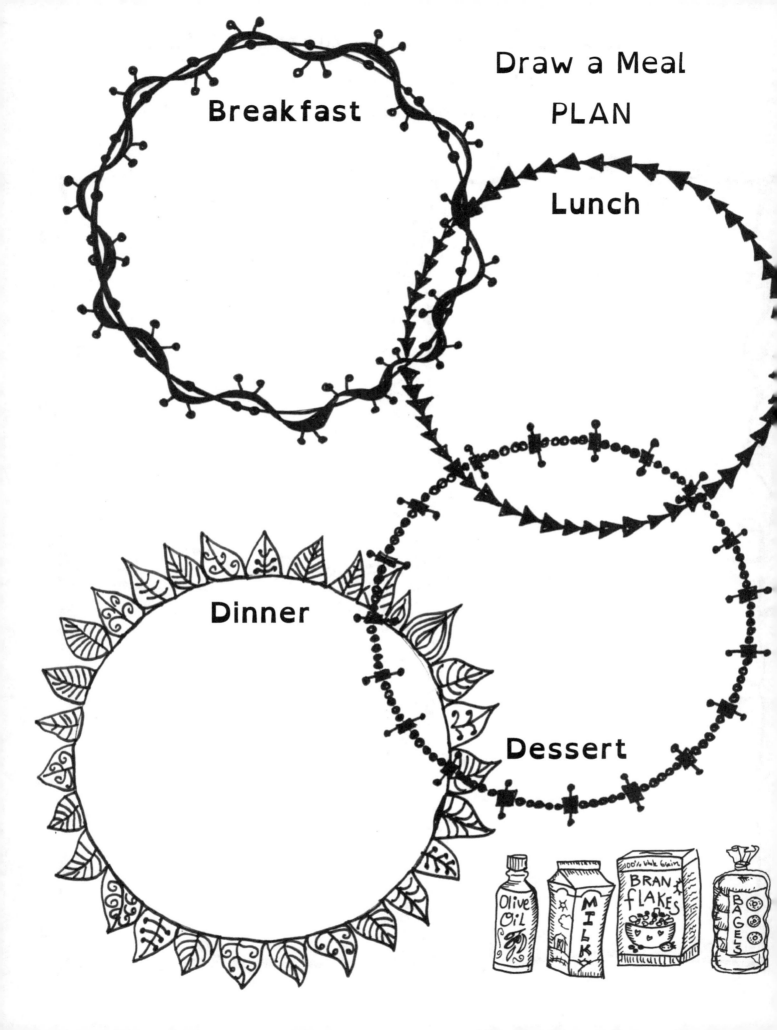

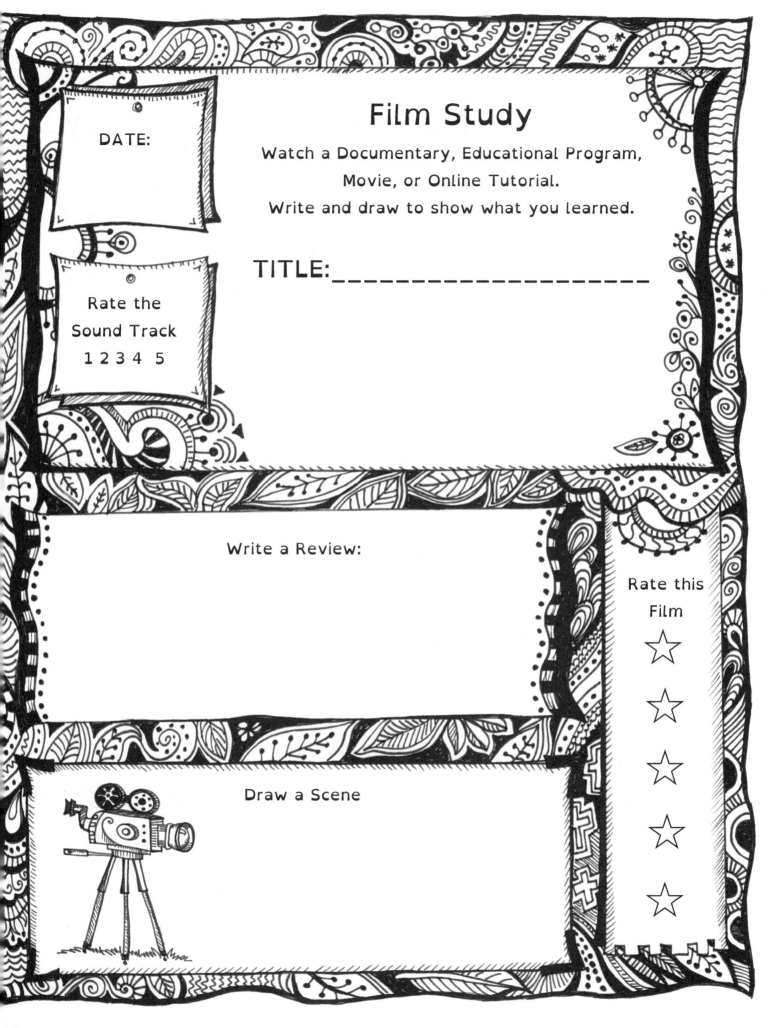

History Time

What is so important about today?

TODAY'S Date:_____

What was the most interesting or important thing that happened in the world on today's date in the past?

Instructions: If today is July 4th, you may write or draw about what happened on July 4, 1776. If today is September 11th, you may write about what happened on September 11, 2001.
(Need help: www.historynet.com/today-in-history)

Past Event:_____
_____
_____
_____

Color the continent where the event happened.

Yesterday's News

What was the most interesting or important thing that happened in the world yesterday?

HEADLINE:

_____

_____

WHO:_____

WHAT:_____

_____

WHEN:_____

WHERE:_____

WHY:_____

_____

_____

Draw It:

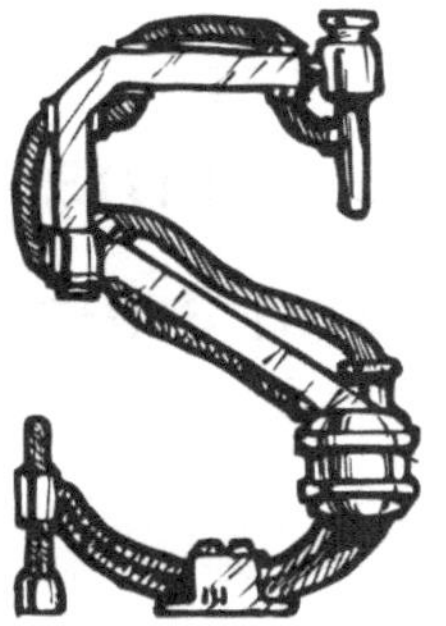

Spelling Time

Find 20 Words with 5 letters each.
Look in your books for words.
Write the words here:

_____   _____
_____   _____
_____   _____
_____   _____
_____   _____
_____   _____
_____   _____
_____   _____
_____   _____
_____   _____

What's My Score?

Try to measure this Animal's abilities and characteristics. Circle a number for each ability. 10 means the animal is the best at a trait. 1 is the lowest score. For example, a cheetah would get 10 in running and a 1 in flying.

Swimming: 1 2 3 4 5 6 7 8 9 10
Jumping: 1 2 3 4 5 6 7 8 9 10
Running: 1 2 3 4 5 6 7 8 9 10
Hunting: 1 2 3 4 5 6 7 8 9 10
Hiding: 1 2 3 4 5 6 7 8 9 10
Climbing: 1 2 3 4 5 6 7 8 9 10
Flying: 1 2 3 4 5 6 7 8 9 10
Gliding: 1 2 3 4 5 6 7 8 9 10
Helping Humans: 1 2 3 4 5 6 7 8 9 10
Building: 1 2 3 4 5 6 7 8 9 10
Traveling: 1 2 3 4 5 6 7 8 9 10

What's My Score? _____

One word that best describes me:

_____

Bible Time

Are you familiar with this story from the Bible?
Tell this story in your own words on the next page.

Emotions & Moods

How are you feeling today? Color the facial expressions to match today's moods.

List 3 things that might help you feel better.

1.
2.
3.

Drawing Time

Look through your library books and find something to draw.

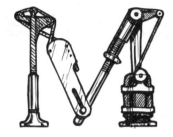

On-Line Math Time

Watch a Math Tutorial on-line
Use this paper to practice what you learn.
Try www.mathtrain.tv or www.khanacademy.org

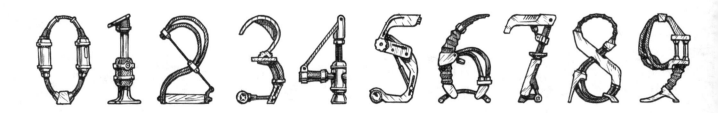

Copywork

Find an interesting paragraph in one of your books and copy it. Be diligent to make your writing look exactly like it does in the book.

TITLE:_____

Listening Time

Listen to an audio book or classical music or ask someone to read a story to you while you color and draw on the next page.

What are you listening to?

_____

Meet the Classics - Copywork

Title:

Tom Sawyer

Author:

Mark Twain

Copy this paragraph onto the next page.

The old lady pulled her spectacles down and looked over them about the room; then she put them up and looked out under them. She seldom or never looked THROUGH them for so small a thing as a boy; they were her state pair, the pride of her heart, and were built for "style," not service -- she could have seen through a pair of stove-lids just as well.

There are many ways to earn money.
Think about the job this person is doing.

I am a _____

Learning About Occupations

What is this person doing?

What skills are needed to do this job?

What would the world be like if no one did this job?

What kind of education does a person need to do this job?

On a scale of 1 to 10 would you like to have this job?

1 2 3 4 5 6 7 8 9 10

There are many ways to earn money.
Think about the job this person is doing.

I am a _____

Learning About Occupations

What is this person doing?

What skills are needed to do this job?

What would the world be like if no one did this job?

What kind of education does a person need to do this job?

On a scale of 1 to 10 would you like to have this job?

1 2 3 4 5 6 7 8 9 10

What books are you reading today?

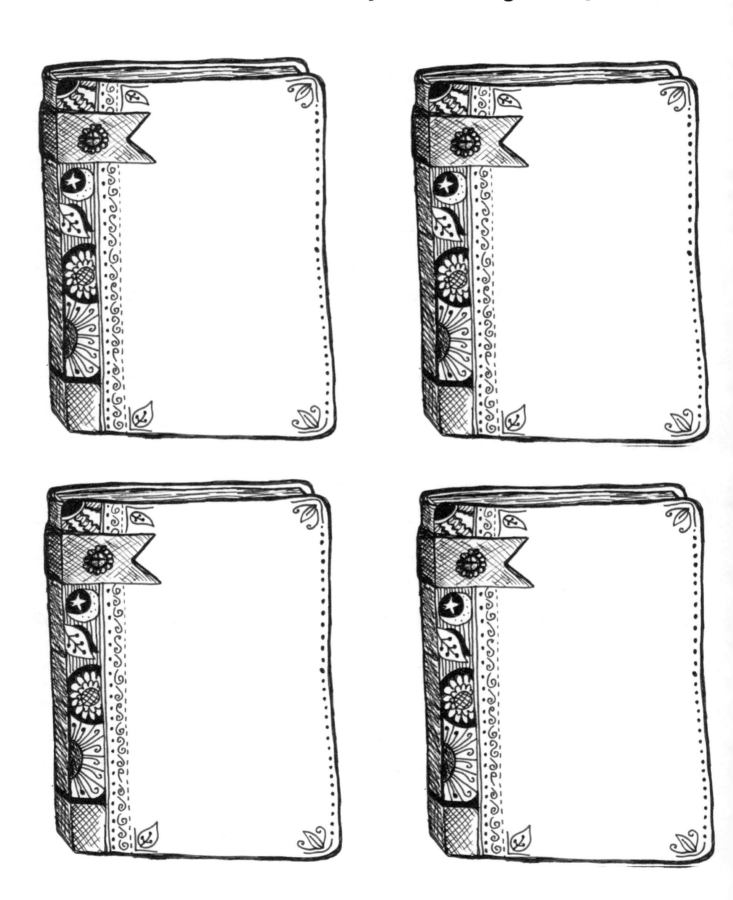

Thinking Time

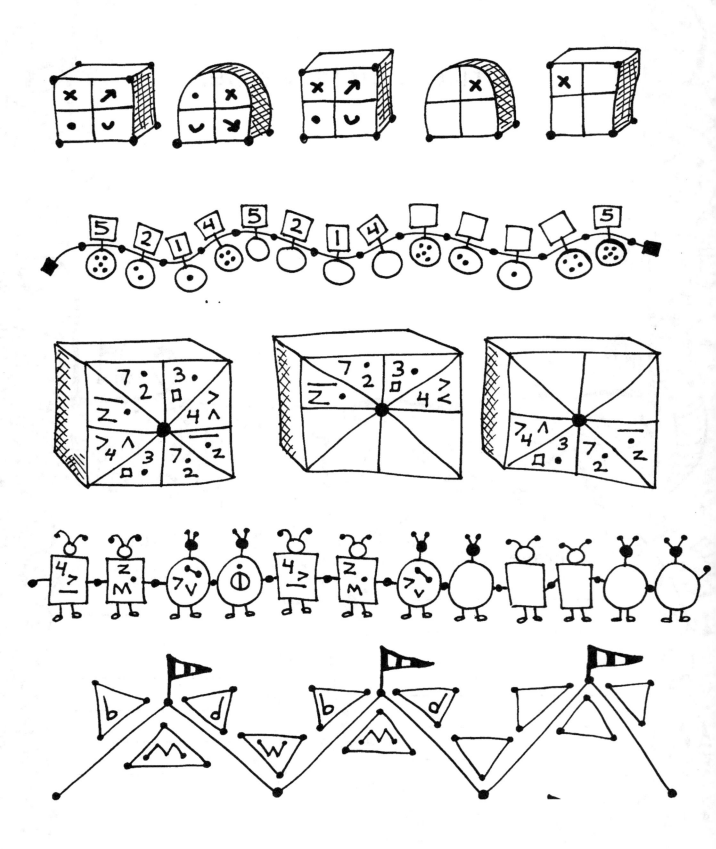

Nature Study

Go outside and make a realistic drawing of something you find in nature.

Story Time - What will happen next?
Draw the rest of the story.

Reading Time- Set a timer for 1 Hour

Read from four books in your stack.
Copy something from each book here.

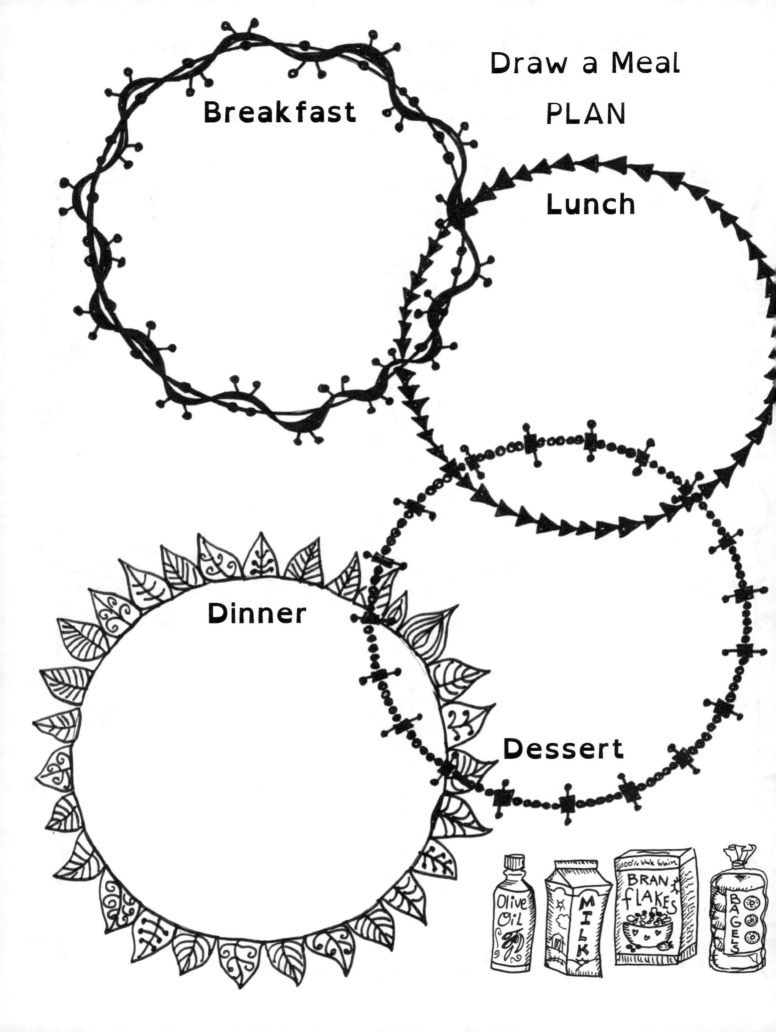

Film Study

DATE:

Rate the Sound Track
1 2 3 4 5

Watch a Documentary, Educational Program, Movie, or Online Tutorial.
Write and draw to show what you learned.

TITLE:_____

Write a Review:

Draw a Scene

Rate this Film
☆
☆
☆
☆
☆

History Time

What is so important about today?

TODAY'S Date:_____

What was the most interesting or important thing that happened in the world on today's date in the past?

Instructions: If today is July 4th, you may write or draw about what happened on July 4, 1776. If today is September 11th, you may write about what happened on September 11, 2001.
(Need help: www.historynet.com/today-in-history)

Past Event:_____
_____
_____
_____

Color the continent where the event happened.

Yesterday's News

What was the most interesting or important thing that happened in the world yesterday?

HEADLINE:

_____

_____

WHO: _____

WHAT: _____

_____

WHEN: _____

WHERE: _____

WHY: _____

_____

_____

Draw It:

Spelling Time

Find 20 Words with 7 letters each.
Look in your books for words.
Write the words here:

What's My Score?

Try to measure this Animal's abilities and characteristics. Circle a number for each ability. 10 means the animal is the best at a trait. 1 is the lowest score. For example, a cheetah would get 10 in running and a 1 in flying.

Swimming: 1 2 3 4 5 6 7 8 9 10
Jumping: 1 2 3 4 5 6 7 8 9 10
Running: 1 2 3 4 5 6 7 8 9 10
Hunting: 1 2 3 4 5 6 7 8 9 10
Hiding: 1 2 3 4 5 6 7 8 9 10
Climbing: 1 2 3 4 5 6 7 8 9 10
Flying: 1 2 3 4 5 6 7 8 9 10
Gliding: 1 2 3 4 5 6 7 8 9 10
Helping Humans: 1 2 3 4 5 6 7 8 9 10
Building: 1 2 3 4 5 6 7 8 9 10
Traveling: 1 2 3 4 5 6 7 8 9 10

What's My Score? _____

One word that best describes me:

_____

Emotions & Moods

How are you feeling today?
Color the facial expressions
to match today's moods.

List 3 things that might help you feel better.

1.
2.
3.

Drawing Time

Look through your library books
and find something to draw.

Bible Time

Are you familiar with this story from the Bible?
Tell this story in your own words on the next page.

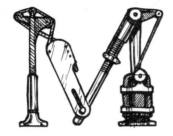

On-Line Math Time

Watch a Math Tutorial on-line
Use this paper to practice what you learn.
Try www.mathtrain.tv or www.khanacademy.org

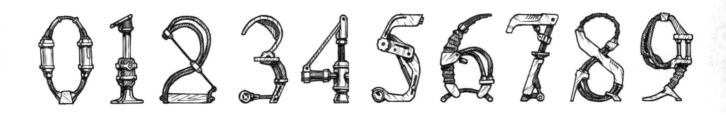

Copywork

Find an interesting paragraph in one of your books and copy it. Be diligent to make your writing look exactly like it does in the book.

TITLE:_____

Meet the Classics - Copywork

Title:

Silas Marner

Author:

George Eliot

Copy this paragraph onto the next page.

In the days when the spinning-wheels hummed busily in the farmhouses-- and even great ladies, clothed in silk and thread-lace, had their toy spinning-wheels of polished oak --there might be seen in districts far away among the lanes, or deep in the bosom of the hills, certain pallid undersized men, who, by the side of the brawny country-folk, looked like the remnants of a disinherited race.

There are many ways to earn money.
Think about the job this person is doing.

I am a _____

Learning About Occupations

What is this person doing?

What skills are needed to do this job?

What would the world be like if no one did this job?

What kind of education does a person need to do this job?

On a scale of 1 to 10 would you like to have this job?

1 2 3 4 5 6 7 8 9 10

There are many ways to earn money.
Think about the job this person is doing.

I am a _____

Learning About Occupations

What is this person doing?

What skills are needed to do this job?

What would the world be like if no one did this job?

What kind of education does a person need to do this job?

On a scale of 1 to 10 would you like to have this job?

1 2 3 4 5 6 7 8 9 10

Libary Books

1. Draw the cover of Four Books that you will read this month.
2. Keep these Books with this Journal.
3. Read from them every day.
4. Use 5 to 10 pages in this Journl everyday.

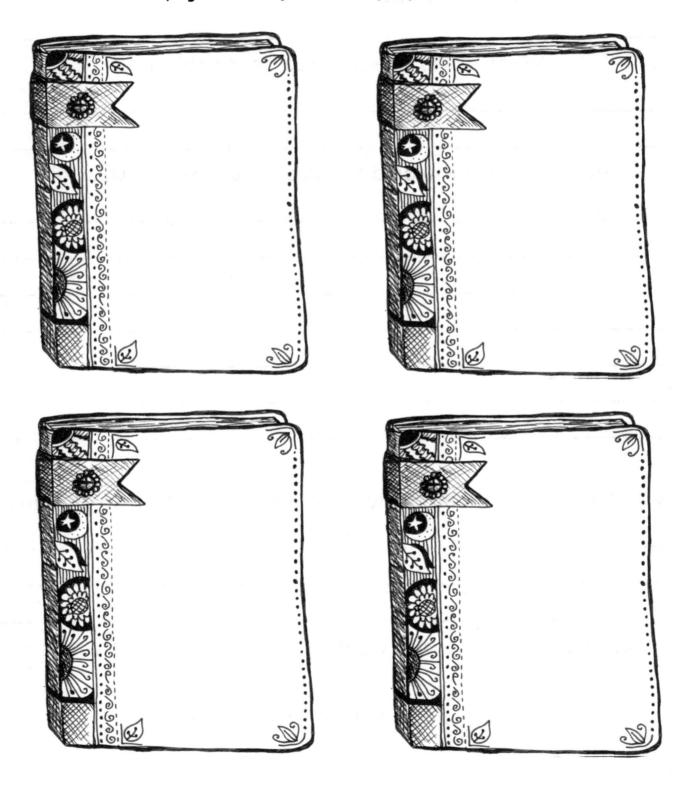

Thinking Time

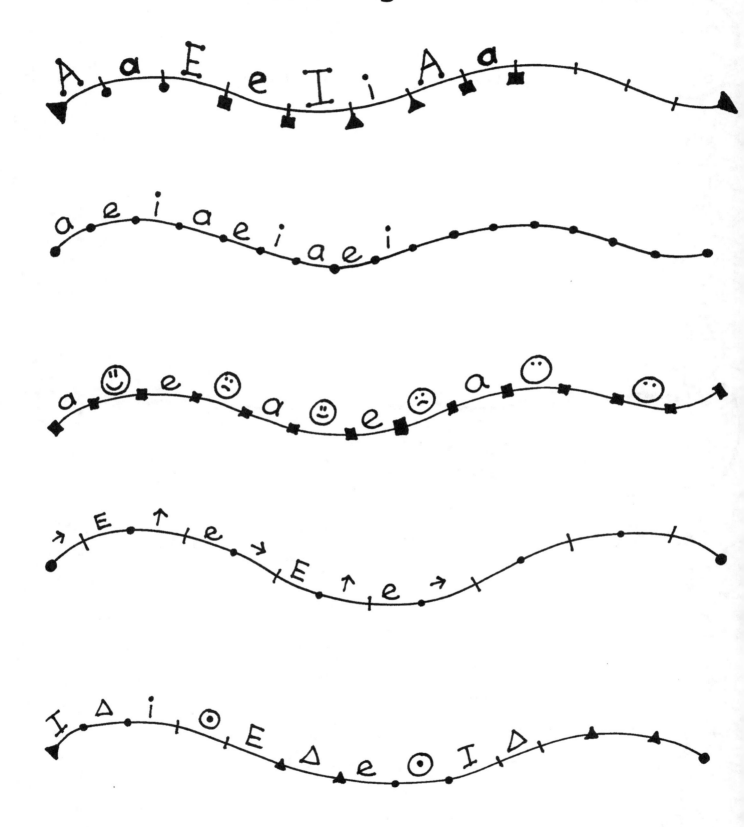

Story Time - What will happen next?
Draw the rest of the story.

Reading Time- Set a timer for 1 Hour

Read from four books in your stack.
Copy something from each book here.

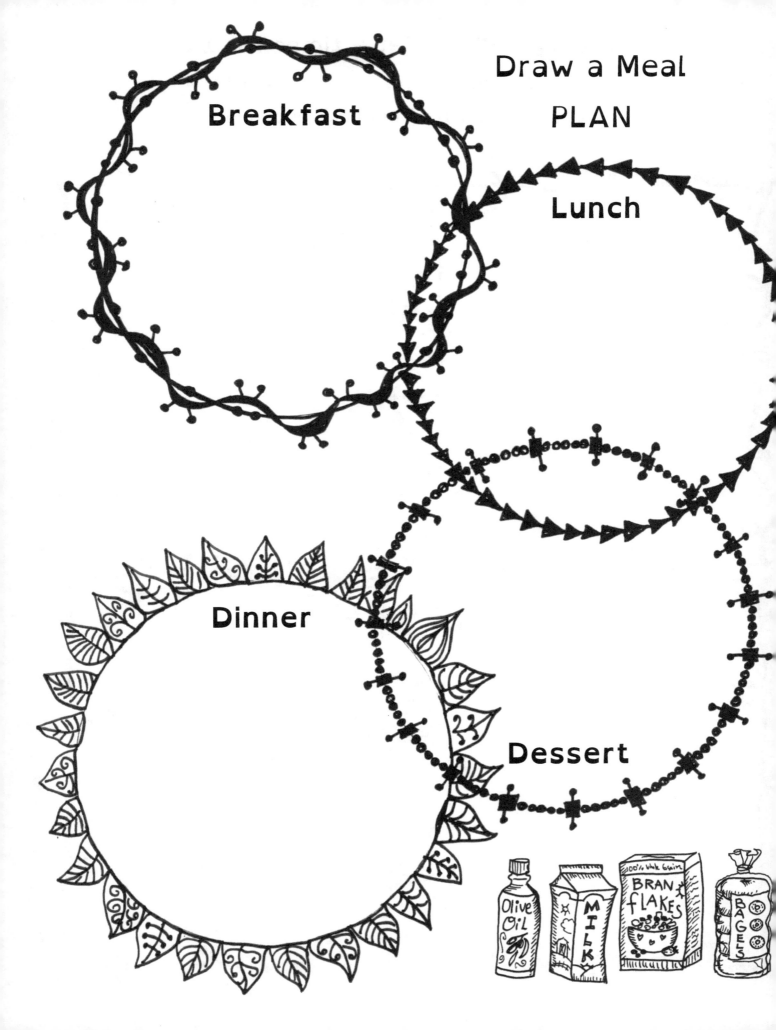

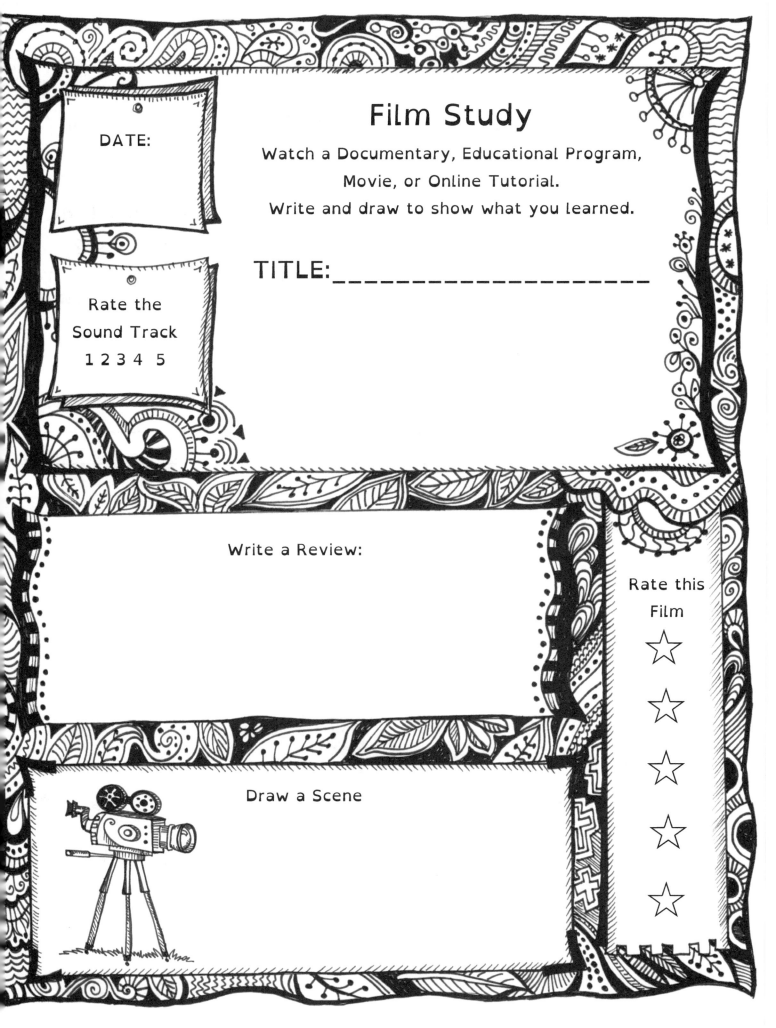

History Time

What is so important about today?

TODAY'S Date:_____

What was the most interesting or important thing that happened in the world on today's date in the past?

Instructions: If today is July 4th, you may write or draw about what happened on July 4, 1776. If today is September 11th, you may write about what happened on September 11, 2001.
(Need help: www.historynet.com/today-in-history)

Past Event:_____
_____
_____
_____

Color the continent where the event happened.

Yesterday's News

What was the most interesting or important thing that happened in the world yesterday?

HEADLINE:

_____

_____

WHO:_____

WHAT:_____

_____

WHEN:_____

WHERE:_____

WHY:_____

_____

_____

Draw It:

Font Writing Practice

ABCDEFGHIJKLMNOPQRSTUVWXYZ

abcdefghijklmnopqrstuvwxyz

ABCDEFGHIJKLMNOPQRSTUVWXYZ

ABCDEFGHIJKLMNOPQRSTUVWXYZ

abcdefghijklmnopqrstuvwxyz

Spelling Time

Find 20 Words with 6 letters each.
Look in your books for words.
Write the words here:

What's My Score?

Try to measure this Animal's abilities and characteristics. Circle a number for each ability. 10 means the animal is the best at a trait. 1 is the lowest score. For example, a cheetah would get 10 in running and a 1 in flying.

Swimming: 1 2 3 4 5 6 7 8 9 10
Jumping: 1 2 3 4 5 6 7 8 9 10
Running: 1 2 3 4 5 6 7 8 9 10
Hunting: 1 2 3 4 5 6 7 8 9 10
Hiding: 1 2 3 4 5 6 7 8 9 10
Climbing: 1 2 3 4 5 6 7 8 9 10
Flying: 1 2 3 4 5 6 7 8 9 10
Gliding: 1 2 3 4 5 6 7 8 9 10
Helping Humans: 1 2 3 4 5 6 7 8 9 10
Building: 1 2 3 4 5 6 7 8 9 10
Traveling: 1 2 3 4 5 6 7 8 9 10

What's My Score? _____

One word that best describes me:

_____

Emotions & Moods

How are you feeling today?
Color the facial expressions to match today's moods.

List 3 things that might help you feel better.

1.
2.
3.

Drawing Time

Look through your library books
and find something to draw.

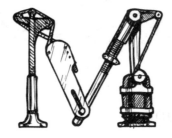

On-Line Math Time

Watch a Math Tutorial on-line
Use this paper to practice what you learn.
Try www.mathtrain.tv or www.khanacademy.org

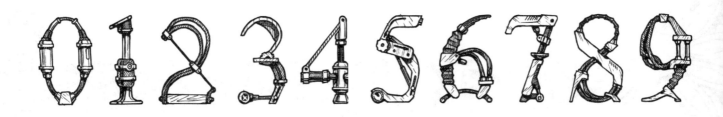

Copywork

Find an interesting paragraph in one of your books and copy it. Be diligent to make your writing look exactly like it does in the book.

TITLE:_____

Bible Time

Are you familiar with this story from the Bible?
Tell this story in your own words on the next page.

Meet the Classics - Copywork

Title:

The Gettysburg Address

Author:

Abraham Lincoln

Copy this paragraph onto the next page.

Four score and seven years ago, our fathers brought forth upon this continent, a new nation, conceived in liberty, and dedicated to the proposition that all men are created equal. Now we are engaged in a great civil war, testing whether that nation, or any nation so conceived and so dedicated, can long endure. We are met on a great battle-field of that war.

There are many ways to earn money.
Think about the job this person is doing.

I am a _____

Learning About Occupations

What is this person doing?

What skills are needed to do this job?

What would the world be like if no one did this job?

What kind of education does a person need to do this job?

On a scale of 1 to 10 would you like to have this job?

1 2 3 4 5 6 7 8 9 10

There are many ways to earn money.
Think about the job this person is doing.

I am a _____

Learning About Occupations

What is this person doing?

What skills are needed to do this job?

What would the world be like if no one did this job?

What kind of education does a person need to do this job?

On a scale of 1 to 10 would you like to have this job?

1 2 3 4 5 6 7 8 9 10

What books are you reading today?

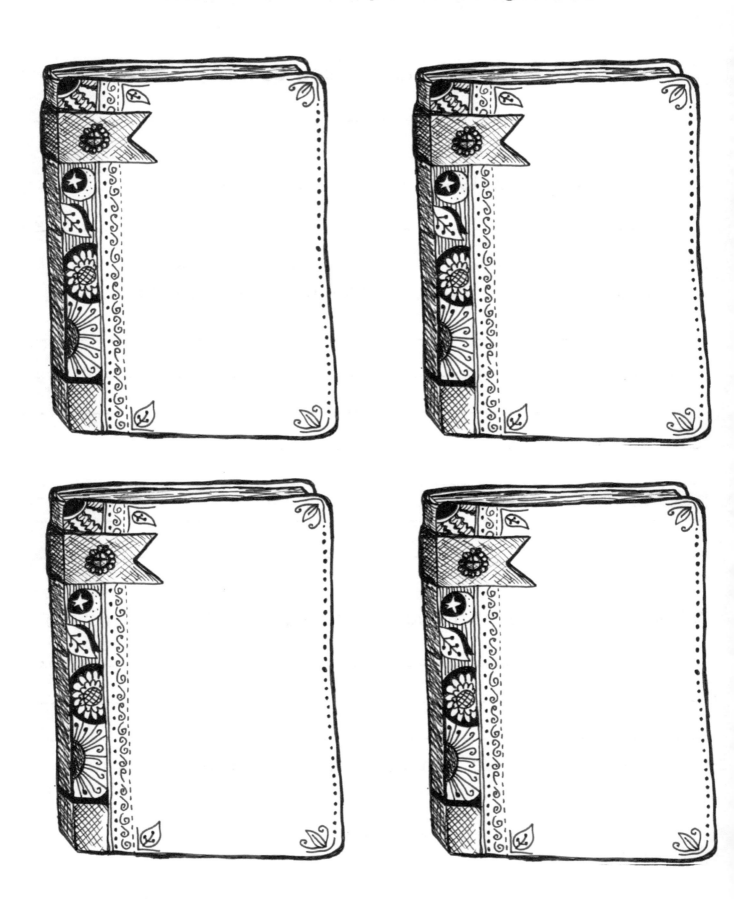

Thinking Time

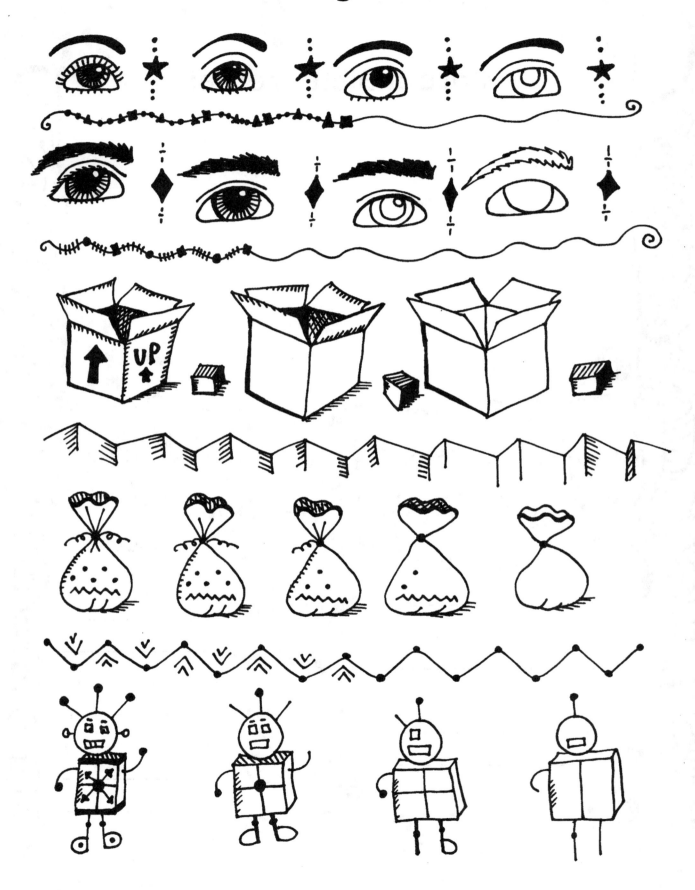

Nature Study

Go outside and make a realistic drawing of something you find in nature.

Story Time - What will happen next?
Draw the rest of the story.

Reading Time- Set a timer for 1 Hour

Read from four books in your stack.
Copy something from each book here.

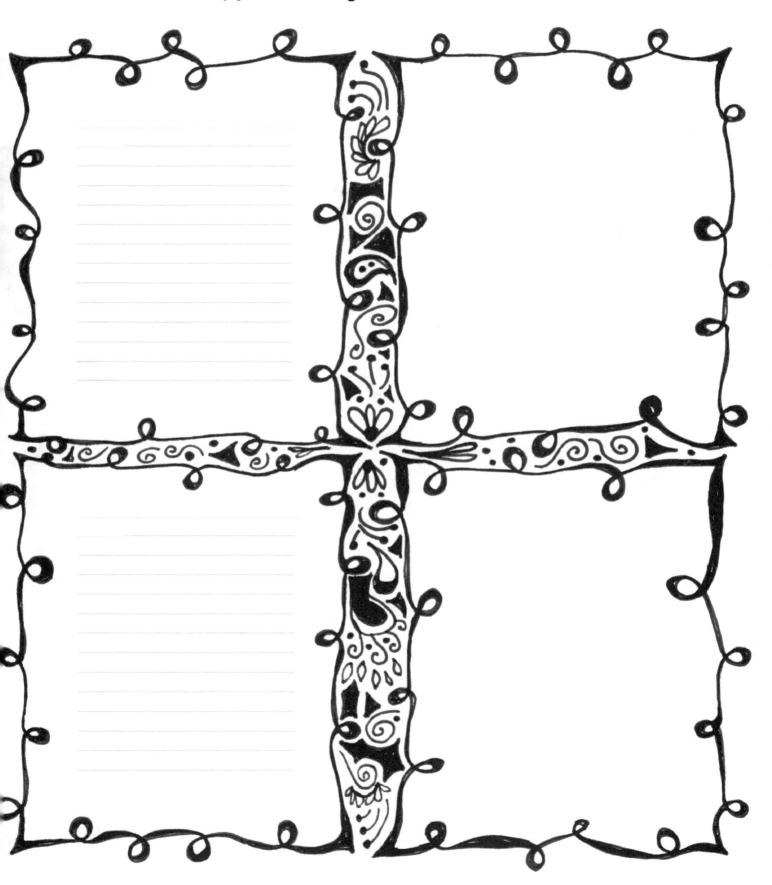

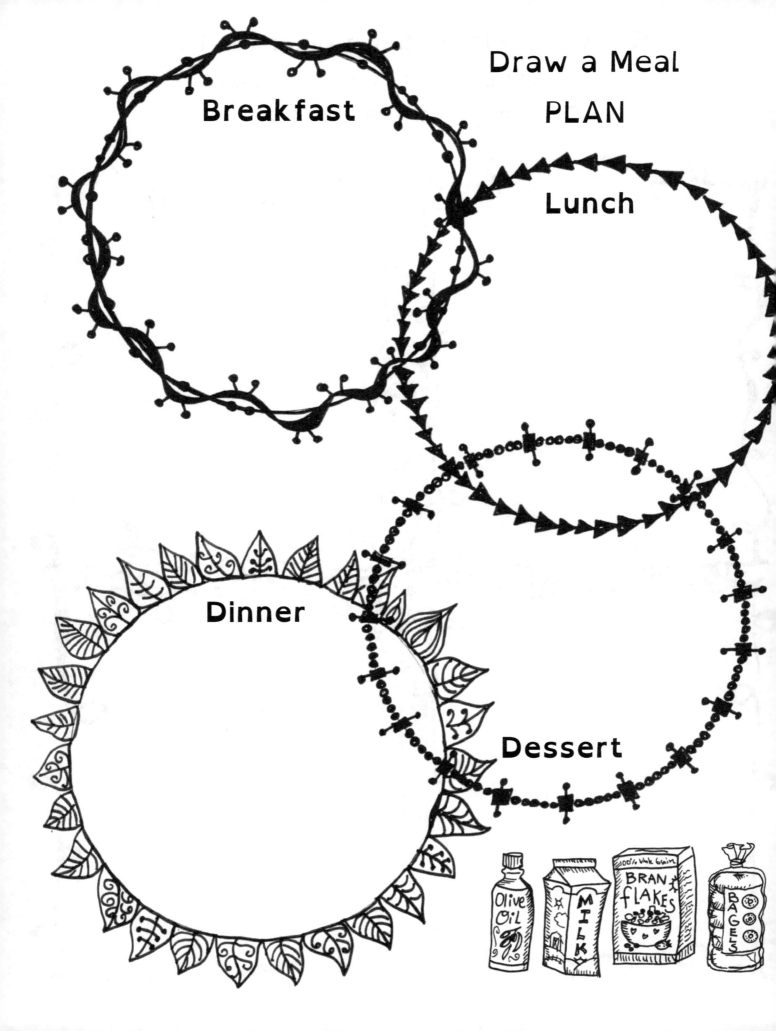

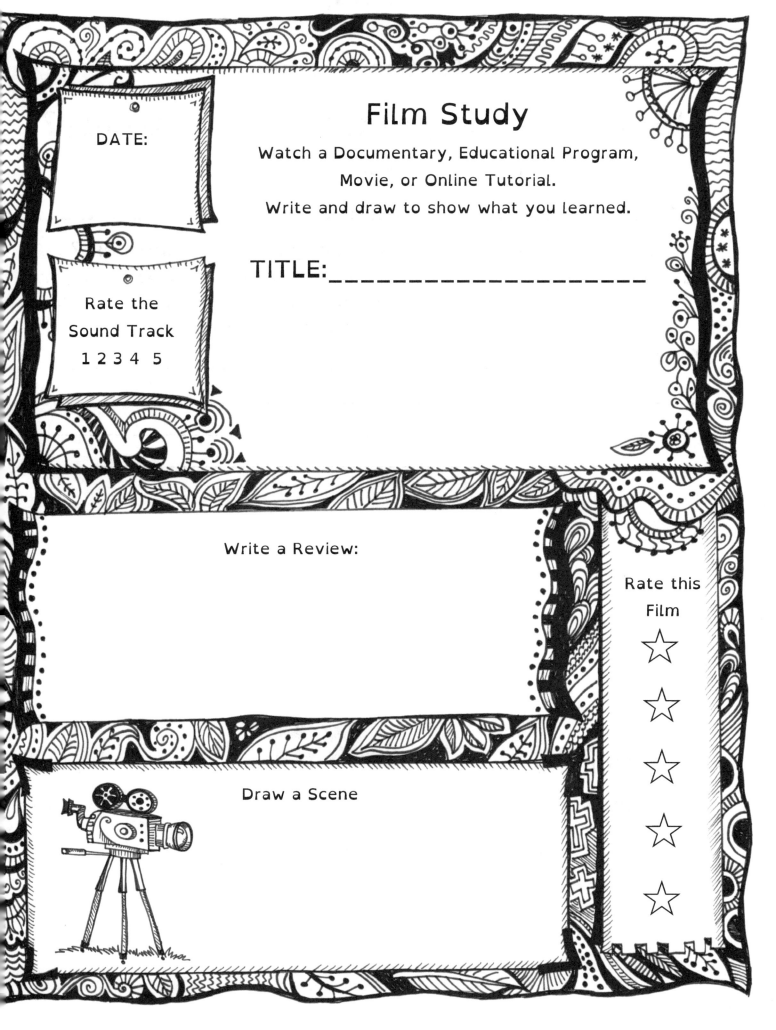

History Time

What is so important about today?

TODAY'S Date:_____

What was the most interesting or important thing that happened in the world on today's date in the past?

Instructions: If today is July 4th, you may write or draw about what happened on July 4, 1776. If today is September 11th, you may write about what happened on September 11, 2001.
(Need help: www.historynet.com/today-in-history)

Past Event:_____
_____
_____
_____

Color the continent where the event happened.

Yesterday's News

What was the most interesting or important thing that happened in the world yesterday?

HEADLINE:

_____

_____

WHO:_____

WHAT:_____

_____

WHEN:_____

WHERE:_____

WHY:_____

_____

_____

Draw It:

Spelling Time

Find 20 Words with 8 letters each.
Look in your books for words.
Write the words here:

Animal Quiz

How much do you know about this animal?

Can you draw the animal's habitat, food and enemies?

What's My Score?

Try to measure this Animal's abilities and characteristics. Circle a number for each ability. 10 means the animal is the best at a trait. 1 is the lowest score. For example, a cheetah would get 10 in running and a 1 in flying.

Swimming: 1 2 3 4 5 6 7 8 9 10
Jumping: 1 2 3 4 5 6 7 8 9 10
Running: 1 2 3 4 5 6 7 8 9 10
Hunting: 1 2 3 4 5 6 7 8 9 10
Hiding: 1 2 3 4 5 6 7 8 9 10
Climbing: 1 2 3 4 5 6 7 8 9 10
Flying: 1 2 3 4 5 6 7 8 9 10
Gliding: 1 2 3 4 5 6 7 8 9 10
Helping Humans: 1 2 3 4 5 6 7 8 9 10
Building: 1 2 3 4 5 6 7 8 9 10
Traveling: 1 2 3 4 5 6 7 8 9 10

What's My Score? _____

One word that best describes me:

_____

Emotions & Moods

How are you feeling today?
Color the facial expressions
to match today's moods.

List 3 things that might help you feel better.

1.
2.
3.

Drawing Time
Look through your library books and find something to draw.

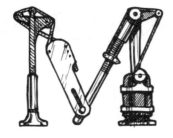

On-Line Math Time

Watch a Math Tutorial on-line
Use this paper to practice what you learn.
Try www.mathtrain.tv or www.khanacademy.org

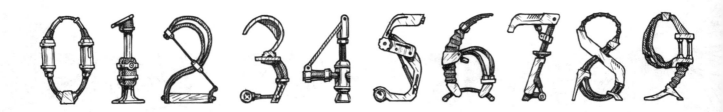

Copywork

Find an interesting paragraph in one of your books and copy it. Be diligent to make your writing look exactly like it does in the book.

TITLE:_____

Meet the Classics - Copywork

Title:

A Christmas Carol

Author:

Charles Dickens

Copy this paragraph onto the next page.

Once upon a time -- of all the good days in the year, on Christmas Eve -- old Scrooge sat busy in his counting-house. It was cold, bleak, biting weather: foggy withal: and he could hear the people in the court outside, go wheezing up and down, beating their hands upon their breasts, and stamping their feet upon the pavement stones to warm them.

There are many ways to earn money.
Think about the job this person is doing.

I am a _____

Learning About Occupations

What is this person doing?

What skills are needed to do this job?

What would the world be like if no one did this job?

What kind of education does a person need to do this job?

On a scale of 1 to 10 would you like to have this job?

1 2 3 4 5 6 7 8 9 10

What books are you reading today?

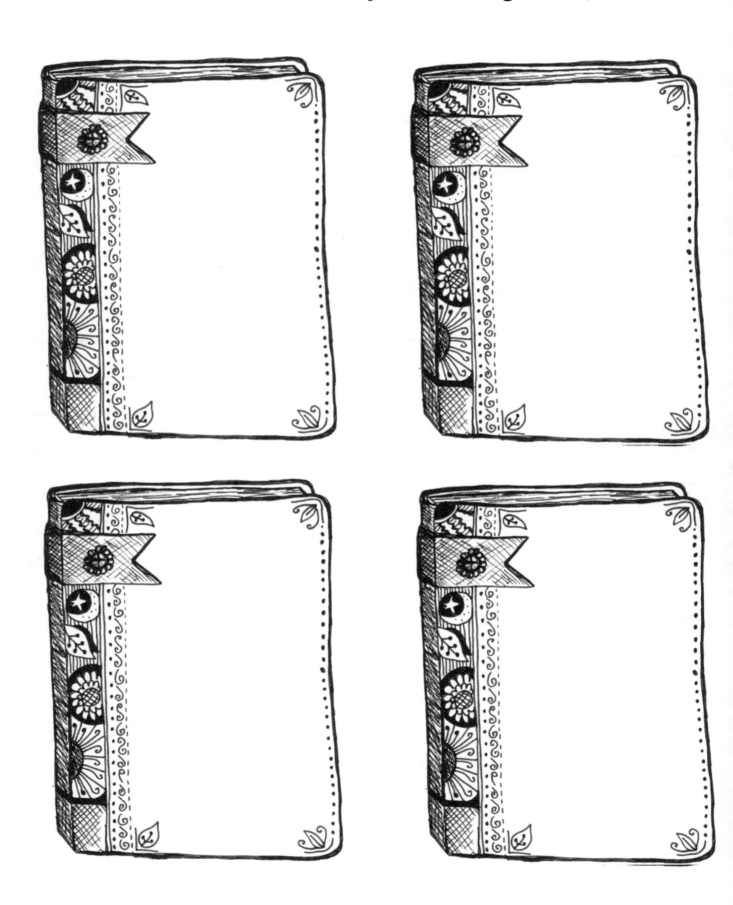

Thinking Time

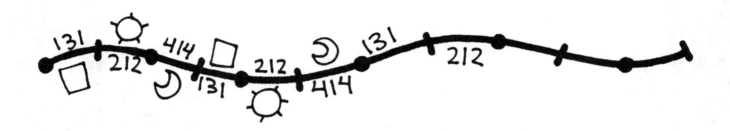

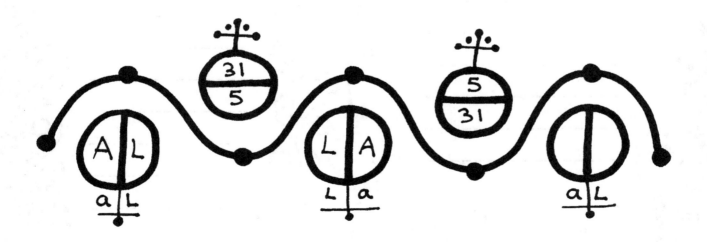

Nature Study

Go outside and make a realistic drawing of something you find in nature.

Story Time - What will happen next?
Draw the rest of the story.

Reading Time- Set a timer for 1 Hour

Read from four books in your stack.
Copy something from each book here.

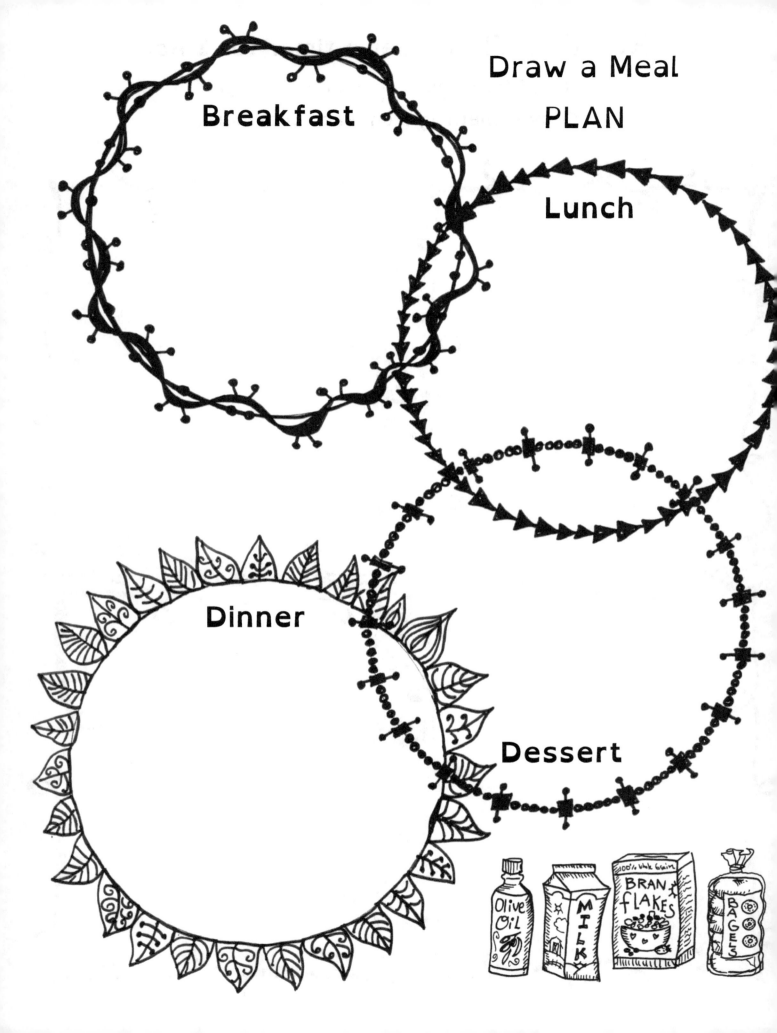

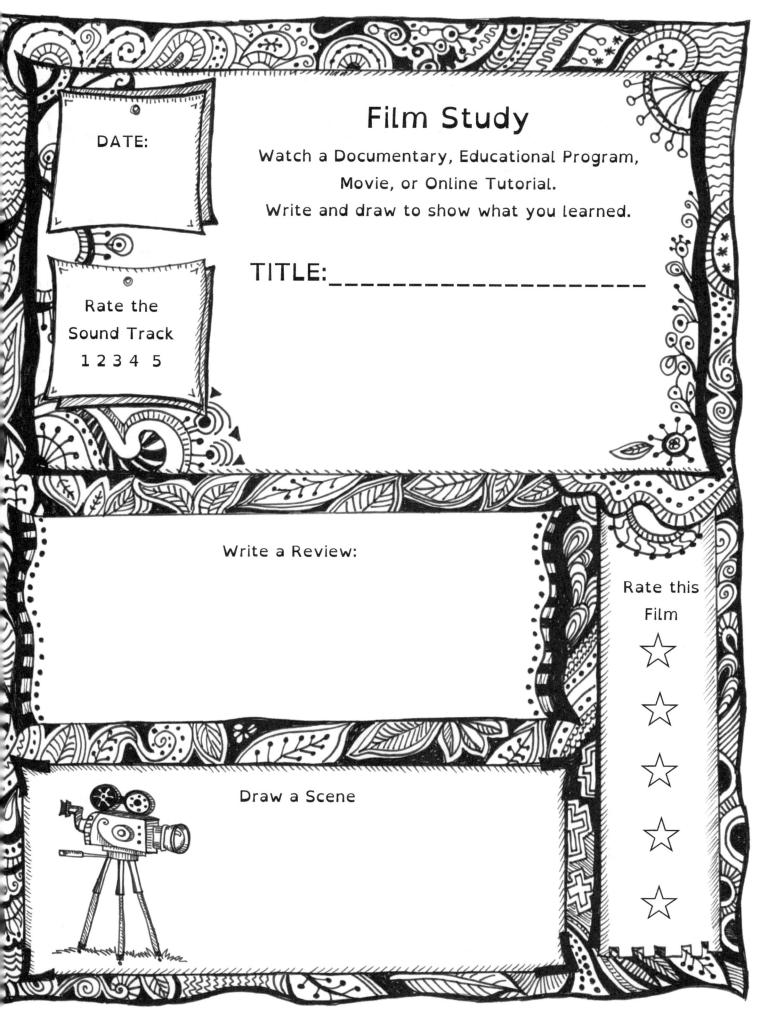

History Time

What is so important about today?

TODAY'S Date:_____

What was the most interesting or important thing that happened in the world on today's date in the past?

Instructions: If today is July 4th, you may write or draw about what happened on July 4, 1776. If today is September 11th, you may write about what happened on September 11, 2001.
(Need help: www.historynet.com/today-in-history)

Past Event:_____

_____

_____

_____

Color the continent where the event happened.

Yesterday's News

What was the most interesting or important thing that happened in the world yesterday?

HEADLINE:

_____

_____

WHO:_____

WHAT:_____

_____

WHEN:_____

WHERE:_____

WHY:_____

_____

_____

Draw It:

Font Writing Practice

ABCDEFGHIJKLMNOPQRSTUVWXYZ

abcdefghijklmnopqrstuvwxyz

ABCDEFGHIJKLMNOPQRSTUVWXYZ

ABCDEFGHIJKLMNOPQRSTUVWXYZ

abcdefghijklmnopqrstuvwxyz

Spelling Time

Find 20 Words with 5 letters each.
Look in your books for words.
Write the words here:

What's My Score?

Try to measure this Animal's abilities and characteristics. Circle a number for each ability. 10 means the animal is the best at a trait. 1 is the lowest score. For example, a cheetah would get 10 in running and a 1 in flying.

Swimming: 1 2 3 4 5 6 7 8 9 10
Jumping: 1 2 3 4 5 6 7 8 9 10
Running: 1 2 3 4 5 6 7 8 9 10
Hunting: 1 2 3 4 5 6 7 8 9 10
Hiding: 1 2 3 4 5 6 7 8 9 10
Climbing: 1 2 3 4 5 6 7 8 9 10
Flying: 1 2 3 4 5 6 7 8 9 10
Gliding: 1 2 3 4 5 6 7 8 9 10
Helping Humans: 1 2 3 4 5 6 7 8 9 10
Building: 1 2 3 4 5 6 7 8 9 10
Traveling: 1 2 3 4 5 6 7 8 9 10

What's My Score? _____

One word that best describes me:

_____

Emotions & Moods

How are you feeling today? Color the facial expressions to match today's moods.

List 3 things that might help you feel better.

1.
2.
3.

Drawing Time

Look through your library books
and find something to draw.

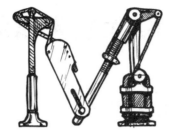

On-Line Math Time

Watch a Math Tutorial on-line
Use this paper to practice what you learn.
Try www.mathtrain.tv or www.khanacademy.org

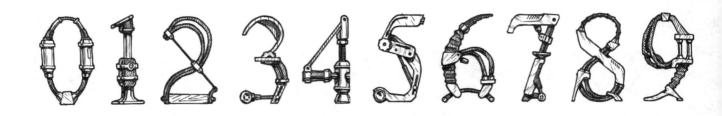

Copywork

Find an interesting paragraph in one of your books and copy it. Be diligent to make your writing look exactly like it does in the book.

TITLE:_____

Meet the Classics - Copywork

Title:

The Adventures of Pinocchio

Author:

C. Collodi

Copy this paragraph onto the next page.

How it happened that Mastro Cherry, carpenter, found a piece of wood that wept and laughed like a child

Centuries ago there lived--

"A king!" my little readers will say immediately.

No, children, you are mistaken. Once upon a time there was a piece of wood. It was not an expensive piece of wood. Far from it. Just a common block of firewood, one of those thick, solid logs that are put on the fire in winter to make cold rooms cozy and warm.

There are many ways to earn money.
Think about the job this person is doing.

I am a _____

Learning About Occupations

What is this person doing?

What skills are needed to do this job?

What would the world be like if no one did this job?

What kind of education does a person need to do this job?

On a scale of 1 to 10 would you like to have this job?

1 2 3 4 5 6 7 8 9 10

There are many ways to earn money.
Think about the job this person is doing.

I am a _____

Learning About Occupations

What is this person doing?

What skills are needed to do this job?

What would the world be like if no one did this job?

What kind of education does a person need to do this job?

On a scale of 1 to 10 would you like to have this job?

1 2 3 4 5 6 7 8 9 10

What books are you reading today?

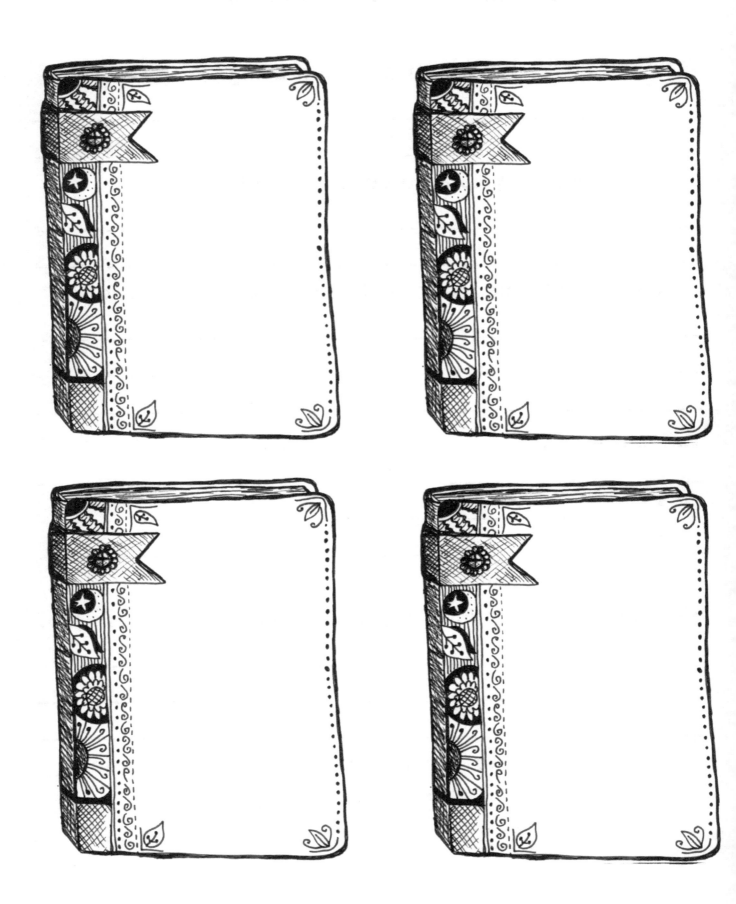

Thinking Time

Story Time - What will happen next?
Draw the rest of the story.

Reading Time- Set a timer for 1 Hour

Read from four books in your stack.
Copy something from each book here.

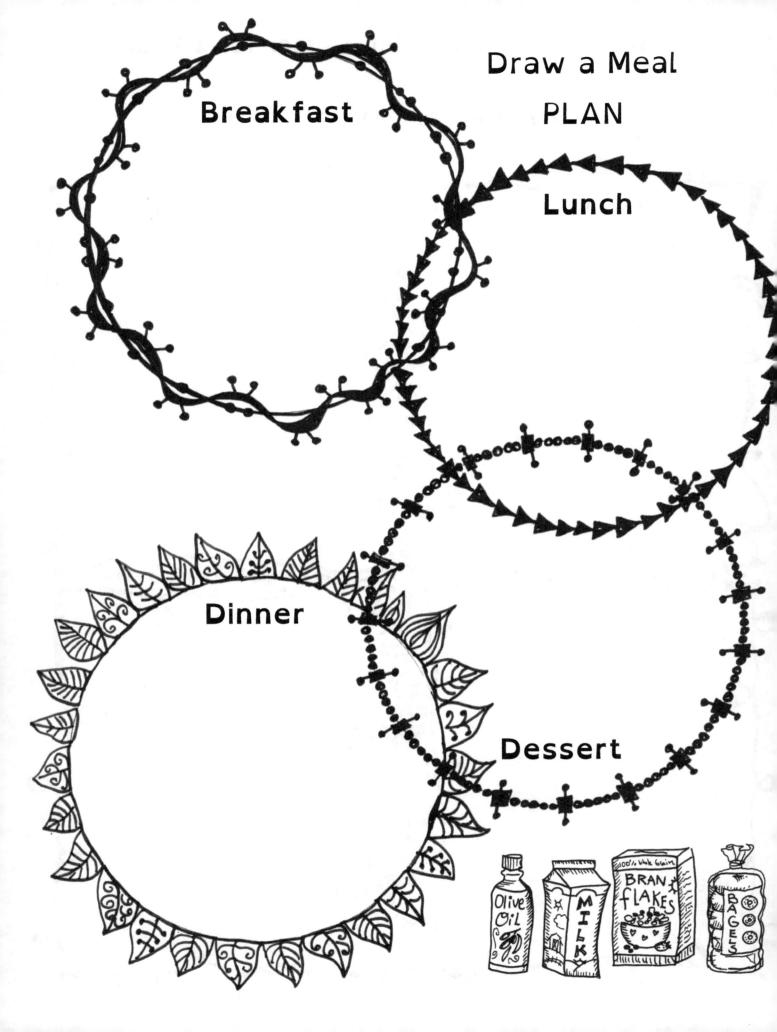

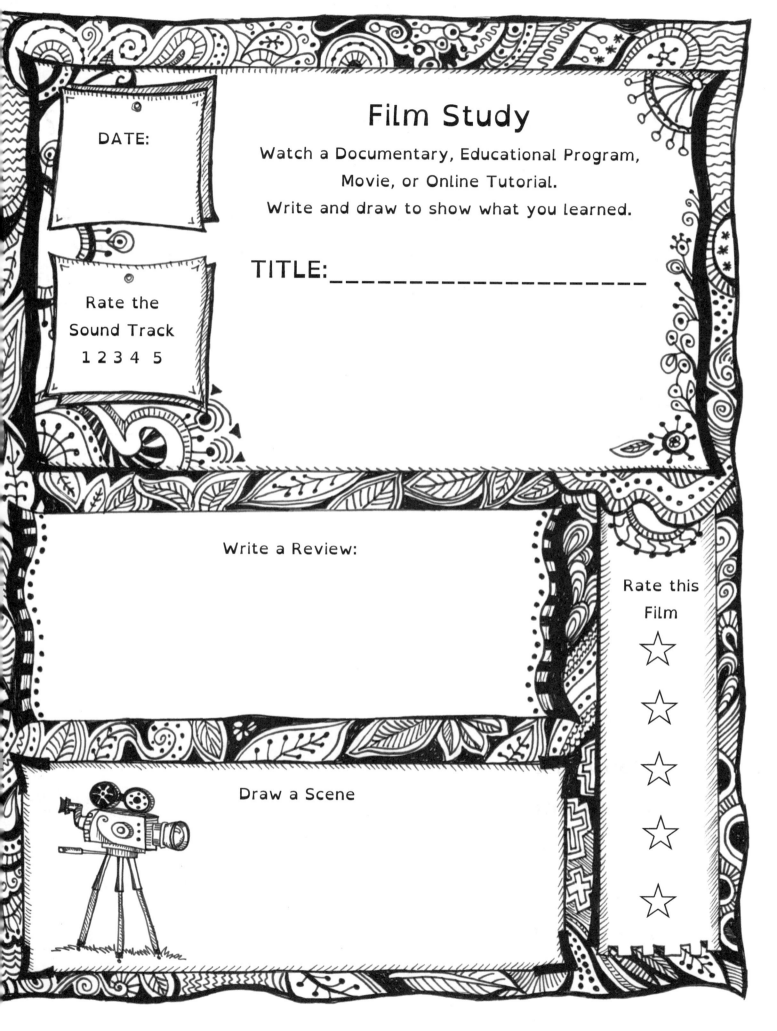

History Time

What is so important about today?

TODAY'S Date:_____

What was the most interesting or important thing that happened in the world on today's date in the past?

Instructions: If today is July 4th, you may write or draw about what happened on July 4, 1776. If today is September 11th, you may write about what happened on September 11, 2001.
(Need help: www.historynet.com/today-in-history)

Past Event:_____
_____
_____
_____

Color the continent where the event happened.

Yesterday's News

What was the most interesting or important thing that happened in the world yesterday?

HEADLINE:

WHO: _____

WHAT: _____

WHEN: _____

WHERE: _____

WHY: _____

Draw It:

Font Writing Practice

ABCDEFGHIJKLMNOPQRSTUVWXYZ

abcdefghijklmnopqrstuvwxyz

ABCDEFGHIJKLMNOPQRSTUVWXYZ

ABCDEFGHIJKLMNOPQRSTUVWXYZ

abcdefghijklmnopqrstuvwxyz

Spelling Time

Find 20 Words with 8 letters each.
Look in your books for words.
Write the words here:

What's My Score?

Try to measure this Animal's abilities and characteristics. Circle a number for each ability. 10 means the animal is the best at a trait. 1 is the lowest score. For example, a cheetah would get 10 in running and a 1 in flying.

Swimming: 1 2 3 4 5 6 7 8 9 10
Jumping: 1 2 3 4 5 6 7 8 9 10
Running: 1 2 3 4 5 6 7 8 9 10
Hunting: 1 2 3 4 5 6 7 8 9 10
Hiding: 1 2 3 4 5 6 7 8 9 10
Climbing: 1 2 3 4 5 6 7 8 9 10
Flying: 1 2 3 4 5 6 7 8 9 10
Gliding: 1 2 3 4 5 6 7 8 9 10
Helping Humans: 1 2 3 4 5 6 7 8 9 10
Building: 1 2 3 4 5 6 7 8 9 10
Traveling: 1 2 3 4 5 6 7 8 9 10

What's My Score? _____

One word that best describes me:

_____

Emotions & Moods

How are you feeling today? Color the facial expressions to match today's moods.

List 3 things that might help you feel better.

1.
2.
3.

Drawing Time

Look through your library books
and find something to draw.

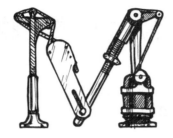

On-Line Math Time

Watch a Math Tutorial on-line
Use this paper to practice what you learn.
Try www.mathtrain.tv or www.khanacademy.org

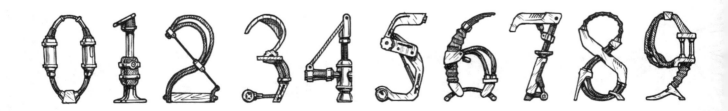

Copywork

Find an interesting paragraph in one of your books and copy it. Be diligent to make your writing look exactly like it does in the book.

TITLE:_____

Meet the Classics - Copywork

Title:

The Adventures of Old Mr. Toad

Author:

Thornton W. Burgess

Copy this paragraph onto the next page.

Old Mother West Wind had just come down from the Purple Hills and turned loose her children, the Merry Little Breezes, from the big bag in which she had been carrying them. They were very lively and very merry as they danced and raced across the Green Meadows in all directions, for it was good to be back there once more.

There are many ways to earn money.
Think about the job this person is doing.

I am a _____

Learning About Occupations

What is this person doing?

What skills are needed to do this job?

What would the world be like if no one did this job?

What kind of education does a person need to do this job?

On a scale of 1 to 10 would you like to have this job?

1 2 3 4 5 6 7 8 9 10

What's My Score?

Try to measure this Animal's abilities and characteristics. Circle a number for each ability. 10 means the animal is the best at a trait. 1 is the lowest score. For example, a cheetah would get 10 in running and a 1 in flying.

Swimming: 1 2 3 4 5 6 7 8 9 10
Jumping: 1 2 3 4 5 6 7 8 9 10
Running: 1 2 3 4 5 6 7 8 9 10
Hunting: 1 2 3 4 5 6 7 8 9 10
Hiding: 1 2 3 4 5 6 7 8 9 10
Climbing: 1 2 3 4 5 6 7 8 9 10
Flying: 1 2 3 4 5 6 7 8 9 10
Gliding: 1 2 3 4 5 6 7 8 9 10
Helping Humans: 1 2 3 4 5 6 7 8 9 10
Building: 1 2 3 4 5 6 7 8 9 10
Traveling: 1 2 3 4 5 6 7 8 9 10

What's My Score? _____

One word that best describes me:

_____

Do It Yourself HOMESCHOOL JOURNALS

Copyright Information

Do It YOURSELF Homeschool Journal, and electronic printable downloads are for Home and Family use only. You may make copies of these materials for only the children in your household.

All other uses of this material must be permitted in writing by the Thinking Tree LLC. It is a violation of copyright law to distribute the electronic files or make copies for your friends, associates or students without our permission.

For information on using these materials for businesses, co-ops, summer camps, day camps, daycare, afterschool program, churches, or schools please contact us for licensing.

Contact Us:

The Thinking Tree LLC
617 N. Swope St. Greenfield, IN 46140. United States
317.622.8852 PHONE (Dial +1 outside of the USA) 267.712.7889 FAX
www.DyslexiaGames.com
jbrown@DyslexiaGames.com

Made in United States
Troutdale, OR
01/23/2025

28279888R00217